Gerald D. Coleman, S.S.

DIVORCE
AND
REMARRIAGE
in the
Catholic Church

PAULIST PRESS
New York ◆ Mahwah

The publisher is grateful to the following for permission to use their material: The Crossroad Publishing Company for permission to quote from Walter Kasper, *Theology of Christian Marriage*, © 1980, Search Press; Paulist Press for permission to quote from "Marriage, Divorce, and Remarriage in the United States," *New Catholic World* vol. 229 (Jan./Feb., 1986); North American Conference of Separated and Divorced Catholics (Kathleen Kircher, executive director, 1100 South Goodman Street, Rochester, N.Y. 14620), for permission to quote from *The Vocation and Mission of the Laity in the Church and Society*. All rights reserved; National Conference of Catholic Bishops for permission to reprint the statement of Bishop Cletus O'Donnell in *Origins* vol. 6, #48 (May, 19, 1977); The Upper Room, for permission to reprint an excerpt from *Prayer, Stress, and Our Inner Wounds*, by Flora Slosson Wuellner. © 1985 by The Upper Room.

IMPRIMATUR: NIHIL OBSTAT:
Pierre DuMaine Maurice F. Shea
Bishop of San Jose *Censor Librorum*

San Jose, California, February 12, 1988

The NIHIL OBSTAT and IMPRIMATUR are official declarations that a book or pamphlet is free of doctrinal or moral error. No implication is contained therein that those who have granted the Nihil Obstat and Imprimatur agree with the contents, opinions or statements expressed.

Library of Congress Cataloging-in-Publication Data

Coleman, Gerald D.
 Divorce and remarriage in the Catholic Church / Gerald D. Coleman.
 p. cm.
 Bibliography: p.
 Includes index.
 ISBN 0-8091-3016-5 (pbk.)
 1. Divorce—Religious aspects—Catholic Church. 2. Remarriage—Religious aspects—Catholic Church. 3. Marriage—Religious aspects—Catholic Church. 4. Pastoral theology—Catholic Church. 5. Catholic Church—Doctrines. I. Title.
BX2254.C65 1988
261.8'3589—dc19   88-23849
                                  CIP

Published by Paulist Press
997 Macarthur Blvd.
Mahwah, N.J. 07430

Printed and bound in the United States of America

Contents

Appreciations

"This work is made possible only with the help of numerous persons, especially those separated and divorced people I have had the honor of learning from over many years. In addition, I acknowledge with thanks seminarians and students at St. Patrick's Seminary and at the Jesuit School of Theology in Berkeley; the invaluable assistance of Mrs. Pam Nurse, the librarian at St. Patrick's; the consistently superb work of the manuscript's typist, Mrs. Jeanne Robles; and the hospitality of the Carmelite Sisters, Carmel, California, who provided the beautiful location for reflecting and writing."

Dedicated, with gratitude and love,
to my parents and my brother, Donald

Introduction

There is little doubt that the question of divorce and remarriage is one of the most difficult and sensitive questions facing the pastoral concern of the Church. On October 25, 1980, at the closing session of the Synod of Bishops in Rome, Pope John Paul II stated:

> *Divorced Catholics who are remarried are not to be considered separated from the Church. . . . By virtue of their baptism, they can and ought to participate in the life of the Church. . . .*

This affirming stance of the Pope—and of the Church—is the basic posture which this present volume intends to study and explicate.

Questions surrounding divorce and remarriage are certainly multiple and very complex. This book will study the questions which are the major pastoral material regarding Catholics who are divorced and remarried. After studying reliable statistics in Chapter One regarding divorce and remarriage, Chapter Two will focus precisely on the theology of Christian marriage which is articulated in the Catholic attitudes and teachings about the marital union. In this regard, we shall see the great complementarity between contemporary theology concerning marriage and canonical legislation as expressed in the 1983 Code of Canon Law.

Subsequent chapters (Three through Eight) will then study specific issues which touch upon, refine, detail and nuance the meaning of Christian marriage: the meaning of "living faith" in order to celebrate the sacrament of marriage; why eucharistic participation is not allowed to those who are divorced and remarried outside the Church; how the "Internal Forum Solution" should be properly understood and pastorally applied; what is the historical meaning of the question of excommunication as understood by the Third Council of Baltimore (1884) and how this understanding has been redefined and rejuvenated in the 1977 statement of the American bishops; how the scriptural materials regarding marriage and divorce greatly affect our pastoral appreciation of the marital union and its occasional deterioration and breakdown; and how the Church has dealt with the question of divorce and remarriage in history.

These areas of study are not meant to simply surface historical and theological insights and interpretations, but also, and perhaps more importantly, to underline the fact that the Church's concern about marriage is indeed twofold: to be a prophetic teacher, and to be a healing reconciler. The Church's pastoral mission regarding divorce and remarriage, then, must mediate both Christ's demanding challenges and his merciful forgiveness and understanding. The Church and its pastoral ministers must perform both of these responsibilities without undermining either; and this is an extremely complicated and sensitive task.

As Chapter One details, it is estimated that during the past decade there were about 120,000 valid Catholic marriages yearly that ended in civil divorce in the United States. In 1971, for example, this was the precise statistic.[1] Although slightly lower, the divorce rate among Catholics in the United States comes relatively close to that of the population at large. This is a problem which the Church in this country has been groping and struggling with for many years. The thrust of this small volume is to help elucidate the various ways in which the Church has wrestled with these issues and continues to do so.[2]

Vatican II in its decree *Gaudium et Spes* teaches that the man and woman who marry "in the Lord . . . are called to live their love in a new and special way with those characteristics of unity and indissolubility which mark every matrimonial pact: marriage, in fact, unites spouses for the whole of their lives with a tie which the sacrament makes sacred."[3]

In studying the various historical, theological and pastoral points in this book, we will highlight the meaning of this "special way" which marks those who enter into the sacrament of marriage. The Church itself sustains supreme regard for this "special way": i.e., the Church jealously guards and proclaims the meaning of Christian marriage, with which married couples "signify and share the mystery of the unity and faithful love between Christ and the Church. . . ."[4]

While this volume deals with major pastoral issues surrounding the question of divorce and remarriage, it does not touch upon some areas of importance which likewise are vital elements in the life and sensitivities of those persons who are divorced and remarried.

One important area of concern not dealt with in this volume is the entire breadth of emotional trauma that touches the life of every divorced individual. The "stages" or "stations" of divorce which are normative for most individuals are important and certainly need careful pastoral sensitivity: e.g., emotional divorce, legal divorce, economic divorce, custody/child visitation divorce, community divorce, and psychic divorce. Although "divorce" seems at first blush to be one experience in the life of an individual, it actually is a composite of all of these six elements, and perhaps others, which sometimes perdure in one way or another for a lifetime.[5]

Another important question not addressed fully in this volume is the problem regarding the nature of a second marriage. In this regard, it is important to remember that a civil marriage normally includes essential human values such as friendship, love, and faithfulness, and these values are often inspired by a genuinely Christian attitude of faith. In his *Theology of Christian Marriage*, Walter Kasper's words are thus instructive:

> *Whenever faith is present in the second, civilly contracted marriage, and is expressed in love and is made effective in penance for the guilt incurred by the breaking of the first marriage, then the second marriage also participates in the spiritual life of the Church. As the one and universal sacrament of salvation, the Church is also at the same time the Church of sinners.*[6]

The following comment of Kasper provides a beautiful form of introduction to the chapters of this book:

> *A broken marriage is not simply cancelled out. It continues to exist. . . . God . . . often writes straight on crooked lines. It is on the basis of this point of view that the Church constructed its order of penance in the past—God does not let us perish after the shipwreck of sin, but He also does not simply allow us to board a comfortable new ship. What He does is to offer us the plank of penance so that we can save our lives. . . . Guilt wounds us and the wound does not simply disappear. It forms a scar and such scars are lasting signs that can hurt again, but they allow us to go on living a humanly fulfilled life that may be all the more mature because of suffering.*[7]

1

Divorce and Remarriage: The People

Available surveys suggest that, by and large, Catholics are much like the population at large.[1] The best available data indicates that during the past fifteen years about a million Catholics have remarried with the Church's blessing. At the same time, about seventy-five percent of remarried Catholics live in presumably invalid second marriages. These divorced and remarried Catholics are not women and men who have rejected the Church's teaching on the permanence and indissolubility of marriage. They are not persons who promote divorce. They almost unanimously are people who profess a high regard for lifelong marriage and generally insist that they would never wish a divorce on anyone.

In addition, data suggests that divorce and remarriage among Catholics does not reflect a lessening of traditional Catholic values among those who have remarried.

As we shall see in Chapter Two, there are multiple factors which suggest themselves as reasons for the widespread divorce and remarriage among Catholics, but certainly there is no reason to indicate that such Catholics have a lesser regard for the Church and family values as any other Catholic. Many commentators cite such contemporary factors as emotional problems, joblessness, addiction, mobility and loss of supportive family relationships, poverty, crime, and effects of Vietnam which contribute toward the fragmentation of family life.

It is a conservative estimate that there are at least six million U.S. Catholics who have been divorced; and since 1978 U.S. diocesan marriage tribunals have processed approximately forty thousand annulment petitions each year. It is estimated that about ten percent of divorced U.S. Catholics have received annulments. It is further estimated that seventy-five percent of divorced Catholics in the United States have remarried or will eventually do so, most without benefit of annulment and without a Catholic celebration of these new marriages.

Despite these statistics, it is important to state that all reliable data supports the conclusion that for Americans, and certainly for American Catholics, the importance of marriage and family life has not in any way decreased, and expectations about marital permanence and stability continue to remain very high, even among young people.

Statistical Data

In "Marriage, Divorce and Remarriage in the United States,"[2] Steven Preister, Executive Director of the National Center for Family Studies at the Catholic University of America, analyzes carefully recent statistical studies regarding marriage, divorce and remarriage in the American population. He indicates that it is a well-publicized fact that there was a rising divorce rate in the United States in the late 1960's and 1970's. At the same time, it is important to realize that this trend reaches much further back than simply the last two decades. In fact, the annual rate of divorce has been rising since 1860, when the U.S. Census first started tracking marriage statistics. It has increased seven hundred percent since 1900. Although the rate fell during the early years of the Depression, it rose again dramatically after World War II.

Preister points out that the rapid rise of divorce in this country seems to be over, at least for the time being. In 1982, for example, the number of divorces in America dropped for the first time since 1962. It fell by 43,000 to 1,170,000. In addition to the 1982 decline in the total number of divorces, the divorce rate per 1,000 people also fell from 5.3 in 1981 to 5.0 in 1982. As Preister indicates, this drop of six percent was more precipitous than any annual decline since those recorded following the steep but temporary surge in marriages and divorces in the aftermath of World War II.

The changing composition of the nation's population doubtlessly is an important factor in understanding these statistics. Young people seeking education and careers are increasingly delaying marriage, resulting in fewer married persons overall, and many of those who wed do so at later ages, likely resulting in more mature relationships.

Data further indicates that if recent rates continue, at least one out of three first marriages entered this year will end in divorce. Statistics seem clear that about forty-five percent of all first marriages and fifty-five percent of all second marriages will likely end in divorce.

It is also significant to realize that marriages are particularly vulnerable to divorce during their early years. Divorces for couples married less than ten years accounted for sixty-four percent of the divorces obtained in 1970, and sixty-seven percent in 1978. Most divorces occur early in marriage, half of them within the first seven years. The average duration of marriages in the United States in 1982 was 9.4 years. Divorces at the older ages are rare: only ten percent of divorcing men and seven percent of divorcing women were fifty years of age and over in 1982.

Preister concludes:

A substantial number of couples who get divorced do it early in their first marriage before having children: the average number of children involved in first divorce in the United States in 1981 was less than one. . . . At the same time, parents no longer feel they should stay together in an unsatisfactory relationship

*for the sake of the children; 60 percent of all divorc-
ing couples have children . . .*

*This is why we have a pastoral concern for preparing
couples adequately for marriage and developing support groups for newly married couples.*[3]

As is evident, the majority of individuals who remarry are
young, and they date and marry relatively soon after divorce,
following a period of cautious experimentation with a new
partner. Interestingly, those who remarry tend to choose other
divorced people as their partners far more often than not.

Almost half of all remarriages take place within three
years of divorce. Seventy-five percent of the divorced begin to
date during their first year of separation and ninety percent do
so by the end of the second year. However, they tend to hold
off on commitments and to experiment in these relationships
in order to ensure that they are making the right decision.

Statistical data further indicates that the probability that a
second marriage will end in divorce is quite high. These marriages are now ending at a slightly higher rate than first
marriages.

Since data indicates that a time of experimentation is in
evidence before remarriage, it is important to analyze briefly
the whole pattern of cohabitation. Living together outside of
marriage is certainly not a new phenomenon, but its higher
incidence as a stage before (re)marriage is new. Once again,
Preister writes:

*The number of couples living together outside of
marriage has increased dramatically. There was a 157
percent increase in unmarried couples living together
in the United States between 1970 and 1980 . . . with
at least one partner previously married in half the sit-*

uations. . . . This followed a similar increase between 1960 and 1970. The number of couples cohabiting is still quite small compared to the entire adult population, but it is growing. However, the accumulated data on this phenomenon are still weak.

McCarthy . . . postulates that cohabitation is not taking the place of formal marriage. Rather, it appears that it is frequently becoming a stage in the marriage process, a stage some couples pass through, or are more likely to pass through, before obtaining a legal marriage. It can even be seen as a sign of a desire for permanence, since more couples want to test a relationship in order to avoid another marital failure.

The practice of cohabitation seems to be concentrated in two groups: the one, the relatively young people around the age of first marriage; the other group is the fairly recently divorced. . . . The young, never married cohabit less than the recently divorced. Cohabitation appears much more widespread among the recently divorced.[4]

A final word regarding this data is of pastoral significance. Divorce and remarriage patterns are obviously having a major impact on U.S. households. Despite variations in the divorce rate, it seems evident that divorce will continue to be the ordinary American solution to intolerable marriages. This presumption sustains a major result for children. In 1984, for example, twenty-six percent of children under eighteen in the United States lived with one parent, compared with thirteen percent in 1970. It was estimated that by 1985, the combined total of single-parent and blended family households would outnumber the total of never-divorced families. Preister concludes:

> *The structure of blended households can be quite complex, since remarriage often involves children from previous marriages. Child Trends (a non-profit research organization) estimates that one child in ten in the United States lives in a blended household. . . . Divorce within the first five years of the establishment of this type of household is estimated at over 44 percent . . . underscoring the difficulties of successfully blending such complex family units.[5]*

Familiaris Consortio

On 22 November 1981, Pope John Paul II issued his exhortation *Familiaris Consortio* (Community of the Family). This exhortation gives greater specificity to the various points which the Pope made at the closing session of the 1980 Synod of Bishops.

In order to properly and pastorally respond to the growing number of divorced and remarried Catholics, it is essential to remember four major points which this exhortation teaches.

First, Catholics who are divorced and who have not remarried enjoy full and complete union with the Church. They are not excommunicated. They may receive the Eucharist.

Second, Catholics who are divorced and remarried (i.e., remarried "outside the Church") should "not consider themselves as separated from the Church, for as baptized persons they can and indeed must share in its life."[6] These persons, in other words, are not excommunicated and should consider themselves members of the whole community of the faithful.

Third, Catholics who are divorced and remarried (i.e.,

remarried "outside the Church") may not participate in the Eucharist because their new relationship, the new marital bond, objectively contradicts the first marital union, which the Church always desires to protect.

As we shall see later, this exhortation clearly teaches that divorced and remarried Catholics (i.e., remarried "outside the Church") are disqualified from eucharistic participation not necessarily because they are living in a state of *subjective* sin.

On the contrary, there are two stated reasons in *Familiaris Consortio* why divorced remarried Catholics cannot participate in the Eucharist:

1. Their new marital bond *objectively* contradicts the first marital union.

2. Simple permission to participate in the Eucharist would inevitably cause scandal among the Catholic faithful.

Fourth, Catholics who are divorced and remarried (i.e., remarried "outside the Church") may not be able to separate for serious pastoral reasons: for example, care for children. Their first responsibility is to bring the first marriage to the Church's marriage tribunal to seek out the possibility of an annulment. If an annulment may not be possible and the couple must continue to live together for pastoral reasons, they are considered a "man and a woman" living together, rather than a "husband and wife," for the first marital union still objectively exists.[7]

Summary

In briefly analyzing the people who experience divorce and remarriage, we have demonstrated that this phenomenon among Catholics clearly does not reflect a lessening of family values. Furthermore, divorce by American Catholics sustains some unique elements different from the general population. Catholics in the United States divorce somewhat less than the population at large.

One significant factor in this statistic may be the support of family values by the extended family and by the Church in such programs as Marriage Preparation and Divorce Support Groups. It is clear that since the 1970's and 1980's, family and parish life programs have been strongly asserting themselves, and this may well make a difference.

It is clear, then, that we urgently need preparation programs for Catholics who are remarrying. In light of the growing number of divorced individuals who live with a new partner as a step toward remarriage, it is also evident that marriage preparation should include not only preparing for a union that has already begun, but also for the change in social status, commitment and family dynamics.

In this light, it is pastorally important to teach clearly the four major points articulated in the exhortation *Familiaris Consortio*. We will carefully analyze these four elements in various parts of this book.

2

Marriage: A Catholic Perspective

Nietzsche called a human being an animal that can promise.[1] This promise tends toward definitiveness. According to Gabriel Marcel, loving another person means telling him or her: you will not die.[2] This concept of "promise" is articulated beautifully in Act II of Thornton Wilder's *The Skin of Our Teeth:*

> *I didn't marry you because you were perfect. I didn't even marry you because I loved you. I married you because you gave me a promise.... That promise made up for your faults. And the promise I gave you made up for mine. Two imperfect people got married and it was the promise that made the marriage.*

As we analyze in this chapter the meaning of marriage from a Catholic perspective, it will be important to carefully discern the meaning of a "promise."

Theology of Christian Marriage

St. Thomas Aquinas wrote his theological synthesis in an attempt to express a Christian view of all human values, including those of marriage. In this regard, he employed St. Augustine's doctrine of the three values *(bona)* of marriage: descendants, mutual love and faithfulness, and the sacramental sign. St. Thomas used these "goods" to express the human dignity of marriage.

Thomas understood human sexuality to be at the service of humankind within marriage by the begetting of descendants. Sexuality was incorporated into personal love and self-surrender by the mutual love and faithfulness of the two spouses. This self-surrender provided a guarantee as well that the wife was valued not simply as a sexual being but as a true partner. Human faithfulness was seen clearly as a sign of God's faithfulness to the covenant in Jesus.

In expressing his synthesis, Thomas concluded that marriage exists only in historical forms and thus it is the nature of marriage to be historical. It is therefore not possible to make any one particular historical or cultural reality of marriage absolute. In light of the various data analyzed in Chapter One, our task in the present age is to do what Thomas Aquinas did so successfully in the high Middle Ages: i.e., to appreciate the doctrine of Augustine in the light of new historical experiences and presuppositions.

As we saw in Chapter One, the presuppositions regarding marriage, divorce and remarriage have greatly changed in recent times. This "change" can be traced back to a number of historical causes.[3]

First, changing attitudes regarding marriage must be seen against the background of the transition of an earlier agrarian society to a modern industrialized and urbanized civilization. In the past, for example, marriage was not simply a private and personal community existing within the framework of a nuclear family based on partnership. Rather, it was also an economic and producing community within the framework of the extended family. On the contrary, in modern technological society, a division has occurred between the sphere of marriage and the family on the one hand, and that of work and professional life on the other. This has led to an extensive collapse of the economic function of marriage and the family, their loss of function with regard to social welfare and care, and their reduction to or concentration on personal relationships.

Second, the recognition of the problem of overpopulation and the evolution of new forms of family planning and birth regulation have furthered the emancipation of marriage and of family life. At least in principle, marriage can be separated from natural conditions of reproduction and procreation.[4]

Third, we have experienced the pivotal discovery of the position of women in society which has dramatically changed our understanding of marriage as a partnership. This recognition had dramatic links with the scientific insight that had been accumulating for almost two centuries and came to its end point in 1875 when it was discovered that new life arose from the fusion of one sperm-cell and one egg-cell and that the woman consequently made an *active* and not simply a receptive contribution to the process of procreation. This discovery has led to a more personalized appreciation of the meaning of marriage and family life.

Fourth, many persons find that they have become increasingly lonely in an increasingly anonymous world, and for them marriage can be a refuge in their search for security. This is one reason why marriage has shown a consistent stability despite all the questionings and threats to which it has been subjected.[5]

Fifth, there is certainly a modern tendency toward emancipation from the compulsions associated with earlier forms of marriage. The so-called sexual revolution, for example, has provided for the possibility of separating fertility and procreation. Certainly modern values such as performance, production, consumption and prestige penetrate into the sphere of marriage and family life.

For these and numerous other reasons, the Church finds itself in a transitional situation. The Second Vatican Council pointed out that humankind was on the threshold of a new dynamic and historically oriented epoch,[6] which has, because of its greater degree of mobility, already led to greater instability in marriage.

Despite twentieth century values as indicated above, marriage has lost, to a greater extent or other, many of its social supports. Civil law, for example, recognizes a relatively wide spectrum of reasons for divorce and, as we have seen, the attitude in society as a whole toward the phenomenon of divorce and subsequent civil remarriage is characterized not simply by tolerance but, in large measure, by indifference and even approval.

It is certainly an urgent pastoral need to minister viably to those who have divorced and married again because of the human suffering experienced in their first marriage. Pastoral sensitivity is also called for regarding those who have found that divorce and remarriage has only led to further suffering, either because of the breakdown of the second marriage, or when new moral responsibilities increase because of the second marriage: for example, children in new blended family households.

In the midst of these many changes, it is important to remember the substantial teaching of *Gaudium et Spes* of the Second Vatican Council (1965). Marriage is here defined as a personal community within which the partners give and accept each other.[7] This more personal view of marriage was likewise taught in the encyclical *Humanae Vitae* (1968). In the first part of this encyclical, marriage is seen in the new light of the Second Vatican Council: i.e., as a personal community.

It is evident, then, that in light of the teachings of *Gaudium et Spes, Humanae Vitae* and *Familiaris Consortio*, there *is* a new point of departure for Christian thinking about marriage: i.e., marriage as mutual love and faithfulness. The essential aspect of the person in marriage should, in other words, be determined not simply naturally, but relationally. As the Council teaches,[8] and as Pope John Paul II has consistently taught:

> The beginning, the subject and the goal of all social institutions is and must be the human person, which for its part and by its very nature stands completely in need of social life.

This personal view of marriage certainly finds an important grounding in the pivotal text of Ephesians 5:21-33. In this text, the covenant between husband and wife in marriage is seen as the image of the covenant between Christ and the Church. The passage closes with the important words, "This is a great mystery and I take it to mean Christ and the Church."

Marriage, then, is a form by means of which God's eternal love and faithfulness, revealed in Jesus Christ, are made historically present. As Walter Kasper points out in *Theology of Christian Marriage*:

> The love that exists between man and wife is rather a sign that makes the reality present, in other words, an epiphany of the love and faithfulness of God that was given once and for all time in Jesus Christ and is made present in the Church.[9]

The love and faithfulness that Christian husbands and wives have for each other, therefore, are not simply the sign and symbol of the love of God; but they are the effected sign, the fulfilled symbol and real epiphany of the love of God that has appeared in Jesus Christ.

This very special sense regarding marriage has led the Second Vatican Council to speak of the family as the "domestic Church."[10] The family thus makes an active contribution to the building up of the Church. This is why married couples have a special gift, a distinctive call within the Church (see 1 Cor 7:14).

In a special way they contribute to both the internal and the external growth of the Church by accepting and bringing up the children whom they are given. They are also able to form "living cells" in the Church by the example of their life together as believers and by the hospitality and openness of their "domestic Church."

It should be clear, then, why the documents of the Second Vatican Council find the more suitable term for marriage as "covenant" rather than "contract" or "institution." Unquestionably, then, in the Catholic perspective marriage is certainly a "special sacrament," thus deserving utmost respect and support.

The Canon Law of Marriage

In the 1917 Code of Canon Law, the following "definition" of marriage can be found:

> *Matrimonial consent is an act of the will by which each party gives and accepts the perpetual and exclusive right over his or her body, for acts which are of themselves suitable for the generation of children (1081:2).*

This canonical definition of marriage stresses the fact that the marriage *is* a contract and is *also* the fulfillment of the contract. The object of the contract is the right over the body of each partner for acts suitable for the generation of children. Consequently, the primary object of the marriage contract is the procreation and education of children (see also 1013:1) and the secondary objects of marriage are mutual help and mutual guarding against concupiscence. In this "definition," the essential properties of marriage are unity and indissolubility (see 1013:2).

As we have already indicated, *Gaudium et Spes,* while not offering a succinct definition of Christian marriage, describes it over several paragraphs (nos. 47-52, especially 48). This description of Christian marriage certainly uses classical terminology but reweaves the Catholic definition of marriage.

In the teaching of the Second Vatican Council and the emerging jurisprudence found in the 1983 Code of Canon Law, the following points are very apparent: marriage is a community of love, rooted in an intimate community of conjugal life and love. Marriage is understood to be the mutual donation of persons rooted in an irrevocable conjugal consent.

Clearly, the "model" of contract is rejected and the model of covenant is consistently followed. In this covenant, persons give themselves to each other, and not merely give the use of their bodies *(Ius in Corpus).*

The crucial passage is found in n. 48 of *Gaudium et Spes:*

For God himself is the author of matrimony, endowed as it is with various benefits and purposes. All of these have a very decisive bearing on the continuation of the human race, on the personal development and eternal destiny of the individual members of a family, and on the dignity, stability, peace and prosperity of the family itself and of human society as a whole. By their very nature the institution of marriage and conjugal love are ordained for the procreation and education of children and find in them their ultimate crown. Thus, a man and a woman, who by the marriage covenant "are no longer two, but one flesh" (Mt 19:6), render mutual help and service to each other through an intimate union of their persons and of their actions. Through this union they expe-

*rience the meaning of their oneness and attain to it
with growing perfection day by day. As a mutual gift
of two persons, this intimate union, as well as the
good of the children, imposes total fidelity on the
spouses and argues for an unbreakable oneness
between them.*

In the 1983 Code of Canon Law, one can clearly discern
three substantial changes that have affected jurisprudence
because of the teaching of the Council:

First, the present Code virtually repeats the words of
Gaudium et Spes, describing marriage as "covenant, by which
a man and a woman establish between themselves a partnership
of their whole life . . ." (1055).

Second, the new Code understands consent as "an act of
the will by which a man and a woman, by an irrevocable covenant, give and accept one another for the purpose of establishing marriage" (1057). The 1917 Code may have presumed
that the spouses intended and were capable of a relationship
marked by mutual love, respect and assistance, but the new
Code directly implies that an assent to these elements is part
of the exchange of persons.

Third, in the new Code, marriage is "ordered to the well-
being of the spouses and to the procreation and upbringing of
children" (1055). Conjugal love thus takes on a new meaning
in that it refers to the mutual sacrificing necessary to bring
about the spouses' well-being.[11]

Summary

The Catholic perspective on marriage understands it to be
"a special sacrament" which sustains the three values of
descendants, mutual love and faithfulness, and the sacramental

sign. The Second Vatican Council, cognizant of the multiple transitions that have occurred which affect the meaning of marriage, has clearly named the marital bond as the "domestic Church." This fact urges the pastoral ministry of the Church to do everything possible to protect this special sacrament and safeguard this domestic Church.

The 1983 Code of Canon Law follows succinctly the theological tradition about marriage in the Council and defines the marital relationship not in the contractual terms of the 1917 Code but in terms of "covenant," as is the language of *Gaudium et Spes*.

3

The Faith Dimension

Context of the Problem

We saw in Chapter Two that numerous historical causes have created a "crisis in marriage." The various causes we studied there, as well as numerous others, have created a new phenomenon in the present secular age that dramatically affects the sacramental meaning of marriage.[1] This new reality facing Christian marriage fundamentally centers on baptized persons who are approaching the Church to witness their marriages but who at the same time profess no evident faith in Jesus Christ, the Church, or the sacramental nature of marriage. This phenomenon has prompted numerous theological inquiries regarding the requirement of faith for the valid reception of the sacrament of marriage.

There are numerous reasons why non-practicing Catholics request marriage in the Church: for example, they are not necessarily non-believers; they like and prefer the setting of the Church for their marriage; their parents or grandparents were married in the Church; they realize that they "have to be" married in the Church.

Concerning this phenomenon, Father Gustave Martelet commented:

> For Christian marriage to be Christian marriage supposes for the spouses a real bond with Christ . . . established by baptism and living faith. . . . The baptized who do not want to believe withdraw them-

selves from the mystery of Christ and the Church and thereby from the sacrament.[2]

It is this phenomenon regarding "living faith" that we propose to study in this chapter.

Theological Issues

Pivotal in this entire discussion is Canon 1055:2. This Canon states: "A valid marriage contract cannot exist between baptized persons without its being by the very fact a sacrament." Consequently, by definition, a baptized couple without living faith requesting a marriage in the Church present a peculiar problem that needs careful study; at the same time, however, should this same couple attempt to contract a civil marriage, their relationship would not be a marriage because it would not be sacramental. This latter problem is an extremely complex one and has to do with the thorny canonical and theological issues regarding the separability of contract and sacrament. We will not study this particular difficulty in this chapter, but rather concentrate on the pastoral dilemma regarding the meaning of "living faith."

The point of departure that is traditionally taken by Catholic canonists and theologians in this regard concerns the identity of the canonically valid and the sacramental marriage.[3] The major objection most often raised regarding the "theory of identity" that every canonically valid marriage is by that very fact a sacramental marriage is that the sacrament is interpreted in an automatic manner.

In this regard, it is vital to recall the traditional teaching of the Church that there can be no automatic sacrament and there can be no sacrament without faith.

A distinction is made in Catholic sacramental theology between the objective validity of the sacrament based on its "objective" expression (traditionally referred to as *ex opere operato*) and a person's fruitfulness in grace which presupposes a certain subjective disposition (normally referred to as the *opus operantis*).

Classical authors pointed out that an integral aspect of the "objective" fulfillment of the sacrament is the presence of at least a minimal intention in the giver and in the receiver of the sacrament, traditionally spoken of as the "intention to do that which the Church does" *(intentio faciendi quod facit ecclesia)*.[4]

In the Canon Law for the Western Church, it is the bride and bridegroom who give each other in marriage and are therefore each at the same time "givers" and "receivers." Consequently, they must both have the intention, as an integral element of their consensus or mutual consent, of entering into their marriage in the Lord. If not, neither a canonically valid nor a sacramental marriage takes place.

What does this intention consist of? From a minimal point of view, it is sufficient for the couple to have a general and direct intention to do what Christians are in the habit of doing in the rite of marriage: i.e., the bride and bridegroom do not need to have the intention of giving and receiving a sacrament of the Church by means of the marriage contract; minimally, it is enough for them to have the intention of marrying in the way in which Christians marry. This "will to marriage" includes the intention to receive the sacrament of marriage as long as it is not explicitly denied.[5]

Obviously, this is a minimal definition of intention, but even according to this minimal definition there can be no valid and sacramental marriage without at least a minimum of faith. Consequently, the Church must do everything possible pastorally, by its proclamation of faith and the context of preparation for marriage and at the marriage ceremony itself, to arouse an understanding in faith of the fullness of the sacrament of marriage. It is pastorally insufficient, if the sacrament is to be fully effective, for the partners to be given a minimal instruction about what constitutes a valid marriage. At the same time, however, in the absence of evidence to the contrary, it must be assumed that couples who want to be married in the Church do have the right intention. A deferment of a Church marriage should be considered only *after* an intensive application of pastoral care.

What seems very clear, then, is that the sacrament of marriage is essentially a mystery of faith and as such requires a certain faith for its reception. The International Theological Commission, a consultative body to the Vatican's Congregation for the Doctrine of the Faith, affirms the need for faith for a fruitful effect of the sacrament of marriage. This commission teaches that where there is no trace of faith and no desire for grace or salvation, then there is "doubt" concerning a truly sacramental intention and thus a sacramentally contracted marriage.[6]

Suggestions on how to determine the presence of a living faith vary.[7] Religious consciousness and awareness on the part of the couple include: affirmation of the Creed and the Ten Commandments; belief in the Lord's Prayer; acceptance of the sacramental nature of the Church; belief in the Trinity, Incarnation and redemption.

Most authors would present a list of criteria that would be necessary for a couple to evidence a "living faith" in order to help them appreciate the fact that they are requesting "a special sacrament" (*Gaudium et Spes*, 48). These criteria are normally outlined in the following hierarchy: belief in God; belief in Jesus Christ; belief in the Holy Spirit; belief in prayer; belief in the sacraments; belief in the Roman Catholic Church; a willingness to participate in a catechesis for marriage preparation which demonstrates an openness to faith and to participation in the Church; a willingness to share the faith with their children; a willingness to share in the Church's worship, especially attendance at Eucharist, which demonstrates an openness to the Church as a community of believers; a willingness to share moral values which demonstrates an openness to the Church as a community of belief; and a willingness to separate for a time before the marriage ceremony should they be living together, which demonstrates an openness to the Church's teachings on human sexuality.

The pastoral point of such a list is for pastoral ministers to carefully determine exactly where they might draw the line and thus indicate that should a couple fall below a certain criterion, they are not yet evidencing sufficient "living faith" to celebrate a sacramental marriage. This judgment is always a very critical and sensitive one, as the Church must avoid at all cost an attitude that makes a person *prove* a readiness to receive the sacrament of marriage. Such "proof" can too easily destroy the meaning of grace within the sacrament of marriage. The new Code does not contain legislation regarding faith, and this absence might well indicate the difficulty of "defining" faith in a juridical context. Pastorally, we might learn something positive from this absence; but it certainly remains the work of pastoral ministers in the Church to further explicate the connection between faith and the sacrament of marriage.

In order to fully appreciate both the meaning and the necessity of "living faith" in order to celebrate fruitfully the sacrament of marriage, the teaching of the International Theological Commission warrants study:

> *Just like the other sacraments, matrimony confers grace in the final analysis by virtue of the action performed by Christ and not only through the faith of the one receiving it. That, however, does not mean that grace is conferred in the sacrament of matrimony outside of faith or in the absence of faith. It follows from this—according to classical principles—that faith is presupposed as a "disposing cause" for*

*receiving the fruitful effect of the sacrament. The
validity of marriage, however, does not imply that
this effect is necessarily fruitful.*

*The existence today of "baptized nonbelievers"
raises a new theological problem and a grave pastoral
dilemma especially when the lack of, or rather the
rejection of, the faith seems clear. The intention of
carrying out what Christ and the Church desire is the
minimum condition required before consent is considered to be a "real human act" on the sacramental
plane. The problem of the intention and that of the
personal faith of the contracting parties must not be
confused, but they must not be totally separated
either.*

*In the last analysis, the real intention is born from and
feeds on living faith. Where there is no trace of faith
(in the sense of "belief"—being disposed to believe),
and no desire for grace or salvation is found, then a
real doubt arises as to whether there is the above-
mentioned general and truly sacramental intention
and whether the contracted marriage is validly contracted or not. As was noted, the personal faith of the
contracting parties does not constitute the sacramentality of matrimony, but the absence of personal faith
compromises the validity of the sacrament.*[8]

While this ITC document affirms that personal faith does
not constitute the sacramentality of marriage, it also makes
clear that its absence certainly compromises the sacrament's
validity. Sacramental theologians thus struggle with the question of whether sacraments are fundamentally viewed as

Christ's free act on us and thus primarily a theocentric activity even though they are efficacious to the extent that they encounter the "living faith" of the believer, or whether the emphasis on this subjective disposition reflects an anthropocentric turn in theology.

The ecclesial dimension of living faith leads to the conclusion that the union of husband and wife is best manifested in a celebration before the community. The sacramental symbolism of Christ and the Church is best expressed in such a context. This value emphasizes the necessary public character of marriage.

In analyzing these and other "Theological Issues," Susan Wood, S.C.L. appreciates certain underlying presuppositions in this whole question.[9]

First, for the fruitful reception of the Sacrament of matrimony, a "living faith" is certainly necessary, at least in some articulated degree. Such faith demands a certain developed religious consciousness which would include a certain amount of theological content, as indicated above.

Second, a Catholic for various canonical and/or pastoral reasons might choose to marry in a nonsacramental manner, but such a choice truly compromises the person's sacramental character of baptism. As Wood writes, " . . . to choose not to participate in God's grace in a sacramental marriage is not a choice in freedom but symptomatic of the distance from true freedom."[10]

Third, to intend to receive a sacrament, it is sufficient to intend by that action what the Church intends by its sacrament. A religious marriage is valid, then, when the prevailing will is to marry, and this will includes those characteristics of marriage intended by the Church: indissolubility, exclusivity, and openness to procreation. When a couple intends such a marriage, they intend to receive what the Church intends as the sacrament. Because the will of the couple is actively involved in this intention, the sacrament is not in any way simply "ceremonial" or "automatic."

Fourth, to intend to receive the sacrament of marriage, minimal faith appears to suffice; pastorally, then, the presumption is made in favor of the faith of the couple. It would be a serious mistake, in other words, to equate nonpractice with nonbelief. Only a direct intention against the reception of any sacrment negates its reception. The absence of faith does not have the same similar negative effect on the reception of the sacrament. St. Thomas Aquinas, for example, indicates that a believer contracts a true marriage with a baptized heretic, but a catechumen, having correct faith but not yet baptized, cannot contract a valid marriage with a baptized believer.[11] In the classical tradition, therefore, the necessary disposition for the valid reception of the sacraments received after baptism is not personal faith, but rather the baptismal character itself. As we have indicated in the case of marriage, the necessary intention for the valid reception of the sacrament includes an intention for indissolubility, fidelity, exclusivity, and openness to children.

Fifth, nonpractice should not be equated with nonfaith, especially when analyzed against Karl Rahner's theology of anonymous Christianity.[12] Rahner convincingly taught that an absence of faith is not easily presupposed when a categorical or propositional expression of faith is lacking. In other words, the nonvalidity of the marriages of baptized nonbelievers cannot and should not be taken for granted. It is true that grave pastoral problems remain, but they cannot be solved without a thorough examination of the theological principles involved.

Sixth, since all of creation has been redeemed, marriage itself can never be considered simply a secular reality. Just as faith can exist before baptism, so is marriage graced before it becomes a sacramental event of grace.[13] Marriage, then, is always a participation in the covenant. As Wood concludes, "If a baptized person refuses to ratify his or her baptism and

wishes to return to a natural order, this person simply cannot
do so, because such an order does not exist."[14]

Summary

In light of these many theological principles, it is important to affirm, when preparing couples for marriage, that one
should *not* begin with the premise that a couple must prove
their faith. On the contrary, ways need to be discovered to
assist the couple to more clearly express the faith that in some
way is already present. In this regard, Wood makes an important point:

> There is a . . . creeping presupposition in some of the
> discussion that the couple request the sacrament of
> the Church and then receive it from the Church as a
> response to their request. This presupposition is par-
> ticularly evident in the marriage program in the Dio-
> cese of Autun. This subtly displaces the minister of
> the sacrament. If the Church "bestows" the sacra-
> ment in response to a request, this presupposes that
> the sacrament is given by the minister of the Church.
> In fact, however, it is the baptized persons contract-
> ing the marriage who minister the sacrament to each
> other. The role of the Church is to witness the
> marriage.[15]

In discerning "living faith," then, the Church in its pastoral ministry should not attempt to impose a "single model"
of what it means to be a Catholic. The Church in this regard
should not be in the business of judging a person's intimate
relationship with God. Marriage preparation programs should

rather be aimed at offering an opportunity for grace to assist a couple to discern if they are sufficiently mature from a religious point of view to enter into a marriage in the Lord. The new Code of Canon Law affirms this point:

> *Pastors of souls are bound in conscience in virtue of their office to fulfill their obligation of providing catechetical instruction on the sacrament of matrimony....*[16]

In assisting a couple to discern the quality of their "living faith," the Church needs to assist them to appreciate more deeply that in celebrating the sacrament of marriage they are not merely being offered, in Bonhoeffer's classical term, "cheap grace":

> *Cheap grace is the preaching of forgiveness without requiring repentance, baptism without Church discipline, Communion without confession, absolution without personal confession. Cheap grace is grace without discipleship, grace without the Cross, grace without Jesus Christ, living and incarnate.... Our humanitarian sentiments made us give that which was holy to the ... unbelieving.*

Celebrating the sacraments with persons who evidence no identifiable indications of living faith teaches them in practice that taking Christ's gifts without concern for the giver is acceptable, thus depriving the recipient of an opportunity to know the joy of true belonging to the Lord and to his Church. The counsel of Pope Paul VI is thus significant: "Nor should anyone pretend that grace supplies for the defects of nature...."[17]

The wedding, then, cannot and should not ever replace the marriage, and the main purpose of marriage preparation programs is to help eliminate "cheap grace" and to positively establish a milieu in which real evangelization can occur: i.e., true discipleship.

4

Eucharistic Participation

Theological Context

In his first encyclical *Redemptor Hominis,* Pope John Paul II wrote of the Eucharist in terms of the sacrament of love, the "center of the life of the people of God."[1]

There is little question that one of the main concerns of and about divorced and remarried Catholics is participation in the Eucharist. Catholics intuit deeply the importance of this sacrament and experience deep loss when they are unable to participate in the Eucharist.

Pastoral experience has demonstrated, for example, that many Catholics in an irregular marriage seek an annulment not so much in order to rectify their irregular situation as to legitimate their participation in the Eucharist.

In May 1977 the bishops of the United States voted to drop the penalty of excommunication for Catholics in an invalid marital union. We will study this question later on in this book. In explaining this decision, the chairman of the Bishops' Commission on Canonical Affairs, Bishop Cletus O'Donnell of the Diocese of Madison, recognized that the problem concerning eucharistic participation remains a difficulty:

> ... *the lifting of the burden of excommunication does not of itself permit those who have remarried after divorce to receive the sacraments of penance and the Holy Eucharist. This last and most difficult question—return to full eucharistic communion—*

can be resolved only in a limited number of instances,
depending on the particular circumstances.[2]

In his article, "Food For Wayfarers,"[3] Joseph M. Powers,
S. J. analyzes two significant theological traditions in understanding properly the meaning of the Eucharist.
First, Powers explains that a more "traditional" view of
the Eucharist emphasizes the real presence of Christ, effected
when a validly ordained priest prays the words of consecration.
In this understanding of the Eucharist, the values of unity,
peace, reconciliation, praise and thanksgiving are seen to be
mediated through the "celebrant" of the Eucharist: i.e., the
priest. The priest is thus understood, Powers explains, as the
minister of the Eucharist and its graces and blessings. In order
to approach the Eucharist and receive its blessings, the faithful
must be "in the state of grace," i.e., free from mortal sin and
worthy to receive the eucharistic Lord.
Second, another theological understanding of the Eucharist clearly appreciates the Eucharist as a sign of unity and
peace in the Church but puts emphasis on the celebration of
the Eucharist on the entire community as the acting subject of
eucharistic prayer. In other words, the gathering of the community for the breaking of the bread is seen as an occasion for
the mutual granting of forgiveness and reconciliation.
Powers points out that Vatican II tends to emphasize this
latter sense of Eucharist. The *Constitution on the Sacred Lit-*
urgy (no. 7) thus teaches:

> *To accomplish so great a work [the praise of God*
> *and the salvation of humanity in Christ] Christ is*
> *always present to His Church, especially in its litur-*
> *gical celebrations. He is present in the Sacrifice of*
> *the Mass, not only in the person of his minister . . .*
> *but especially in the eucharistic species. By his power*

he is present in the sacraments. . . . He is present in his word, since it is he himself who speaks when the holy Scriptures are read in the Church. Lastly, he is present when the Church prays and sings, for he has promised: "Where two or three are gathered together in my name, there I am in the midst of them."

In it [the liturgy] full public worship is performed by the mystical body of Jesus Christ, i.e., by the head and his members.

In addition, no. 11 of this Constitution emphasizes that it is from the Eucharist that the faithful receive the power to live their Christian life in the world. Powers thus concludes:

In other words, the "substance" which is to be changed is not only the substance of bread and wine. The "substance" which is changed in the eucharistic community is the entire life of the community which gathers for celebration of the Eucharist.[4]

It is evident in these two theological traditions that the Eucharist is understood, first, as a "sign" of unity in the Church, and, second, as a source for unity within the Church. Vatican II affirms in the *Constitution on the Sacred Liturgy* that the Eucharist is both the *goal* of life for every believer as well as the *source* of the possibility for living more fully the Christian life.

In a special way, then, the Eucharist is the unique sacrament which nourishes the value of Christian living and consistently initiates the Christian along the way of the community's historical process of being the Church in the world.

It is thus not surprising that Catholics intuit and appreciate a tremendous understanding of and need for the Eucharist, even when they themselves are not in full unity with the teachings of the Church—for example, persons who are divorced and remarried outside of the Church.

Some authors affirm the reception of Communion by a divorced, remarried person where his or her first marriage is irretrievably lost, but where one or both parties have entered into a stable new marriage where he or she is faithful to obligations which remain from the first marriage, such as raising children in the faith or financial support. Many authors affirm that such persons should be offered the Eucharist as a spiritual resource to assist them in the demands of the new marriage. Clearly this affirmation rests on the theological tradition represented by the "second" point of view spoken of above. In this chapter, we must carefully analyze this teaching.

Canonical and Theological Questions

Canon 897 teaches:

The most venerable sacrament is the blessed Eucharist, in which Christ the Lord himself is contained, offered and received, and by which the Church continually lives and grows. The Eucharistic sacrifice, the memorial of the death and resurrection of the Lord, in which the sacrifice of the cross is forever perpetuated, is the summit and source of all worship and Christian life. By means of it the unity of God's people is signified and brought about, and the building up of the body of Christ is perfected. The other sacraments and all the apostolic works of Christ are bound up with, and directed to, the blessed Eucharist.

Clearly, this canon appreciates the Eucharist as *both* the sign of unity within the Church, as well as the source for unity in the Church.

Canon 912 further teaches: "Any baptized person who is not forbidden by law may and must be admitted to Holy Communion." A critical question here, of course, is to carefully understand what category of persons are "forbidden by law" to participate in the Eucharist. A certain reply comes in canon 915:

> *Those upon whom the penalty of excommunication or interdict has been imposed or declared, and others who obstinately persist and manifest grave sin, are not to be admitted to Holy Communion.*

Who are those persons who "obstinately persist and manifest grave sin"? To reply carefully to this question, we must remind ourselves of the teaching of *Familiaris Consortio* (1981) of Pope John Paul II, as explained in Chapter One. We there explained that this papal exhortation explains that Catholics who are divorced and remarried (i.e., remarried "outside the Church") may not participate in the Eucharist because their new relationship, the new marital bond, objectively contradicts the first marital union, which the Church always desires to protect.

This exhortation thus concludes in this regard that if such persons are repentant for whatever contribution they have made to the breakdown of the first marriage, they *may* receive the Eucharist if they are willing to live a life of continence.

This teaching is not meant to be punitive but is meant to safeguard the indissolubility of the marital bond. In other words, the Church recognizes the stability of the first marriage bond as perduring until such time that an annulment process indicates that such a bond *de facto* never existed. Despite the counsel of some writers as mentioned above, then, the official teaching of the Church recognizes the persons living sexually in a second marriage as manifestly dishonoring the unity of the first marital bond. Unless these persons are willing to live as "brother and sister," therefore, they may not participate in the Eucharist, since the Eucharist is first of all the *sign* of unity in the Church.

The *Constitution on the Sacred Liturgy* affirms the importance of the Eucharist:

> *Mother Church earnestly desires that all the faithful be led to that full, conscious and active participation in liturgical celebrations which is demanded by the very nature of the liturgy. Such participation by the Christian people . . . is their right and duty by reason of their baptism.*[5]

The Council's *Pastoral Constitution on the Church in the Modern World* furthers this teaching by focusing on the Eucharist as true "strength for life's journey."[6] The importance and centrality of the Eucharist are thus a clear and direct teaching of the Church; and it is with great reluctance that the Church feels compelled to limit this eucharistic participation. The 1979 pastoral letter of the Italian Episcopal Conference attempts to explain why it is necessary at times to limit eucharistic participation in order to uphold the value of faithfulness:

> *The Church . . . asks remarried divorcees to keep alive the dialogue with God: in humble and confident prayer they will be able to find spiritual help for their situation of life.*
>
> *. . . the Church is called to live its obedience to Christ. . . . The Church, in fact, knows that it is the*

custodian and faithful administrator of the signs and means of grace that Jesus Christ has entrusted to it.

Thus the pastoral problem of a possible sacramental life for the remarried divorcees can be tackled and solved rightly only in the perspective of the faithfulness of the Church to its Lord.

The sacramental celebration is the peak moment in which the Church carries out its mission of proclaiming the Gospel by building up the community of believers. For this reason the sacraments are the signs of the faith of the Church.

The non-admission of remarried divorcees to the sacraments does not signify at all a punishment, but only a love which wishes to remain authentic because it is inseparably bound up with truth.

The Church cannot deceive remarried divorcees, treating them as if they were not in a situation of moral disorder.[7]

Some literature prefers to name this "situation of moral disorder" as "sin." This designation is not a helpful one, however, as it too easily gives the impression that the person living in an irregular marriage is in the state of subjective sin. The Church does not teach this. It is thus important to recall the traditional distinction between objective and subjective sin. The point here is that because the person chooses to live in a situation contradictory to the Gospel, he or she is living out a moral disorder. Whether this objective situation is also coupled with subjective sin depends totally on the conscience of the individual.

For pastoral reasons, it is essential to realize that the Church is limiting eucharistic participation for those who are in an irregular union because the bond established with the former spouse is presumed to be valid and thus presumed to still be in existence. The teaching here of Pope Paul VI is helpful:

> . . . *a marriage exists at the moment when the spouses express a juridically valid matrimonial consent. This consent is a will-act which establishes a contract (or a conjugal covenant, to use the phrase preferred today). In an indivisible moment of time it produces a juridical effect, namely, an existing marriage as a state of life. Once the moment is passed, the wills of the consenting partners have no power to affect the juridical reality they have brought into being. Consequently, once the consent has produced its juridical effect, it automatically becomes irrevocable and lacks power to destroy what it created.*[8]

In limiting eucharistic participation to those in an irregular union, then, the Church is not making a discernment about an individual's personal guilt or the state of his or her conscience. Rather, the Church is maintaining that such a couple is living in a situation which *imperfectly* symbolizes the unity of Christ and his Church and thus this "moral disorder" does violence to the meaning of indissolubility. The Church, therefore, is not here making a statement about a person's personal worthiness. This point is of utmost significance. On 25 October 1980, at the closing session of the Synod of Bishops in Rome, Pope John Paul II affirmed this point:

> *Divorced Catholics who are remarried are not to be considered separated from the Church. . . . By virtue*

*of their baptism, they can and ought to participate in
the life of the Church. . . .*

Theological Analysis

In light of canonical jurisprudence and the teachings of
Pope John Paul II at the close of the 1980 Synod as well as in
the exhortation *Familiaris Consortio* (1981), it is clear that
there are three major arguments in the Church's official teaching against eucharistic participation for those in an irregular
marriage.

First, these persons are living a "moral disorder" and thus
from an objective point of view their living-situation contradicts their first marital bond.

Second, because of this fact these persons imperfectly
symbolize unity within the Church; and unity in the sacraments presupposes full unity in faith and discipline (the "first"
theological tradition presented at the beginning of this
chapter).

Third, if such persons in an irregular marriage are given
encouragement or permission to participate in the sacraments,
others will conclude that it is not wrong to remarry after
divorce; the question here is one of scandal.

In these three major arguments of the Church, it is clear
that the questions of indissolubility and the reception of the
Eucharist are inseparable issues.

There are some theologians and writers who would affirm
the possibility of some persons living in an irregular marriage
to participate in the Eucharist.[9] These authors would support
a cautious admission of some divorced/remarried Catholics to
the Eucharist if certain conditions are fulfilled:

1. The first marriage is irretrievably lost.
2. Present methods of official reconciliation are unavailable
   (e.g., an annulment is not possible).

3. The parties have indicated by their lives that they desire to participate fully in the life of the Church.
4. There are solid grounds for hope of stability in the second union.

These authors certainly affirm the importance and significance of the indissolubility of the marriage bond. They understand this indissolubility, however, as engendering an absolute and serious moral obligation or "ought" which at times is violated through sinfulness and/or personal weakness. These authors certainly stress that no bond exists once the marriage is truly "dead." The present pastoral difficulty in the Church is that this teaching contradicts the official teaching of the Church, as already seen in the example from the teachings of Pope Paul VI.

The writers who affirm the possibility of some persons in an irregular marriage to participate in the Eucharist emphasize the concept of marriage as explained in *Gaudium et Spes,* no. 48: Marriage is a "community of love, an intimate partnership." This "community of love" generates the bond between the two people (as different from simply their consent). This couple sustains the moral obligation to continually grow into a more total "community of love."

Gaudium et Spes, no. 48, affirms this point when it teaches: "As a mutual gift of two persons, this intimate union, as well as the good of the children, imposes total fidelity on the spouses, and argues for an unbreakable oneness between them." These authors tend to *stress* the capacity for intimate partnership as that which constitutes the true marital bond: i.e., the spouses are bonded to each other and ought not to allow this bond to be broken but must do everything possible to protect it when it is imperiled.

As we have already seen, the Church officially teaches that the *consent* of the partners creates an irretrievable bond that is not subject to the later will-acts of the couple themselves. On the contrary, the authors that we are here summarizing stress that when the capacity to live a "community of love" is authentically gone, is irretrievably lost, the "bond" is no longer there. The logical conclusion to such an argument is that a subsequent marriage cannot be a violation of a bond that *de facto* no longer exists because it is irretrievably lost.

Needless to say, these questions are extremely complicated and sensitive and need further and very careful analysis by competent scholars as well as the magisterium of the Church.

Summary

The Eucharist is understood by the Church as both the sign and the source of unity. The Church limits participation in the Eucharist only with regret. This chapter has demonstrated that the Church officially understands those living in an irregular union to objectively contradict the indissolubility of the marital bond established in the first commitment of marriage. This bond continues in existence since the parties' consent gave birth to this bond.

A number of writers are questioning this approach to the meaning of the marital union, and stress that where a capacity for a "community of life and love" is no longer present, neither is the bond itself.

It is of utmost importance for the pastoral unity of the Church to underline and affirm the Church's official teachings on this subject. It creates pastoral havoc when certain ministers within the Church encourage participation in the Eucharist for those living in an irregular union, while other ministers do not do this because of the Church's official teachings. It is always important, of course, to protect the unity of the Church and to be sensitive to the well-being of all of the faithful.

Certain conclusions seem clear:

First, the Eucharist should never be thought of as a reward for perfect adherence to moral and juridical standards. While it is true that the situation of the divorced, remarried Catholic is ambiguous juridically, it does not follow that the person is necessarily unworthy or improperly disposed for the Eucharist. Canon Law affirms, for example, that persons are excluded from the Eucharist only if they demonstrate open and willful disregard for the institution of marriage, a contempt not sustained by the majority of divorced, remarried Catholics.[10]

Second, while the objective situation of the divorced, remarried Catholic might be one of "disorder" in light of the Church's teaching about indissolubility, this does not mean that such persons sustain a sinful attitude or will: i.e., they are not necessarily unworthy *in conscience*. As we have seen, the Church permits some couples in an irregular union to remain together (e.g., in the brother/sister relationship) and thus their marital situation is not intrinsically evil. This point carries an important theological affirmation, especially in light of the points we discussed in Chapter Three regarding the sacramental nature of all of creation.

While it may well be the case that many persons living in an irregular union sustain no personal sinful attitude or will, it must be restated that the reason that the Church excludes such persons from the Eucharist is for *objective* reasons: i.e., their second union violates the meaning of indissolubility.

Third, the divorced, remarried Catholic is a full member of the Church and is invited to participate in the Church as fully as possible. These persons are not cut off from the graces which the Church offers; they are encouraged to participate in Mass and other liturgical celebrations.

Fourth, the Church must demonstrate a pastoral care for the well-being of the entire ecclesial community. In any pastoral decision concerning admittance of a divorced, remarried

Catholic to the Eucharist, then, the Church's official teaching on this question must remain normative. Once again, this teaching must not be interpreted as punitive but rather as an approach which is grounded in faithfulness to the Gospel and to the Church's tradition.

Fifth, in the documents of Vatican II, the Eucharist is never presented as a reward for perfect adherence to moral and juridical standards; rather, it is presented as a celebration of a pilgrim Church. The use of the deprivation of the Eucharist as a penance is, therefore, a complete falsification of the meaning of the Eucharist. It is thus necessary to properly understand and pastorally present the Church's position on why those in an irregular union are excluded from the Eucharist.

To present the reasons for this exclusion as a "punishment" is to totally falsify the Church's authentic teaching on this question; and failure to provide true pastoral assistance needed by those struggling to reconcile their personal situation with the radical demands of the Gospel is a true scandal in the Church.

The following statement of the International Theological Commission is instructive:

> Without refusing to examine the attenuating circumstances and even sometimes the quality of a second civil marriage after divorce, the approach of the divorced and remarried to the Eucharist is plainly incompatible with the mystery of which the Church is the servant and witness. In receiving the divorced and remarried to the Eucharist, the Church would let such parties believe that they can, on the level of signs, communicate with him whose conjugal mystery they disavow on the level of reality. To do so would be, moreover, on the part of the Church to declare itself in accord with the baptized at the

moment when they enter or remain in a clearly objective contradiction with the life, the thought and the being itself of the Lord as spouse of the Church. If the Church could give the sacrament of unity to those who have broken with it on an essential point of the mystery of Christ, it would no longer be the sign of the witness of Christ but rather a countersign and a counterwitness. Nevertheless, this refusal does not in any way justify any procedure that inflicts infamy and which contradicts in its own way the mystery of Christ toward us sinners.[11]

5

The Internal Forum Solution

The Meaning of Forum and Good Faith

The notion of a forum as a special place goes back to the early days of civilization. As a juridical term, it comes from the usage to which the place which it designated was put, e.g., the Forum Romanum, in an age when religion, political life, and law intermingled. Etymologically, the word implies a fencing which both protects and separates.[1]

This etymology gives rise to the distinction in Church teaching concerning the "external forum" and the "internal forum."

The external forum of the Church concerns the governance of the Church; the focus here is on the community of the Church itself and its relational life. The "common good" is the emphasis, and the ordinary instrument of the external forum of the Church is law and juridical certitude.

On the other hand, the internal forum of the Church is concerned directly with the sanctification of souls (the *cura animarum*) and deals with an individual's conscience.

An example of the external forum of the Church is the canonical process of annulment, and an example of the internal forum process in the Church is the sacrament of reconciliation.

The Council of Trent desired to establish a nonsacramental internal sphere; the distinction thus developed between the "internal forum" and the *forum poenitentiale*. In either case, however, jurisdiction in the internal forum had no efficacy in the external forum. This is the major historical reason why it is pastorally important to always consider the "common good" when making decisions in the internal forum.

Both fora in the Church have a great deal to do with the "good faith" of an individual. Good faith has a very specific meaning in Church teaching and refers to a prudent judgment that one truly possesses (or "owns") something: i.e., a persuasion of lawful ownership. Good faith is lawful in conscience inasmuch as it excludes one from sin.

This matter of good faith is so intimately linked to the notion of internal forum that it is important here to look further into the complexities regarding "good faith."

A person sustains "good faith" if he or she *truly believes* (a) the truth of the matter in point and (b) that he or she is not in sin because of such a belief. What is an example?

A Jewish person has been married and then divorced. This person then married a Catholic. Neither the Jewish person nor the Catholic had any notion at all that the first marriage of the Jewish person prevented a marriage in the Catholic Church. In other words, they *truly believed* that the first marriage was "invalid" in the eyes of the Catholic Church, and that since they were divorced, each party would now be free to marry in the Catholic Church (or anywhere, for that matter).

When the Catholic and the Jewish person were preparing for their wedding in the Catholic Church, the person preparing them asked, "Have you been married before?"

The Jewish person replied "no," honestly believing that as far as the Catholic Church is concerned, he was not truly married before. In "good faith," then, he answered "no."

To complete this example: a year after this marriage in the Catholic Church a priest learns that the Jewish person had been married before to another Jewish person. In the eyes of the Church, this former marriage was a valid marriage. What should the priest do?

If the priest feels that there is really no possibility of changing the present situation (i.e., it is unreasonable to think that this couple can now separate), and that telling the couple the "objective" truth of their situation would entail putting them in "bad faith," his *obligation* is to remain silent. In other words, the priest should never put another person in bad faith.

In this example, the priest is recognizing the "good faith" in the conscience of the Catholic and the Jewish person, and the priest sustains no moral responsibility to place them in bad faith. In this case, the priest should not hinder the Catholic party from receiving the Eucharist. Why? Because he has made a prudential judgment in the "internal forum."

Good Conscience

Many authors and ministers in the Church frequently use the term "good conscience" in a manner synonymous with "good faith."[2] In the vocabulary of "good conscience" the following distinction is normally made.

First, "good conscience" refers to those who are morally certain that their first marriage was *invalid:* i.e., their first marriage was never a marriage at all. It was undermined, for example, by emotional illness or serious personality defects from the start.

Second, "good conscience" refers to those who are morally certain that their first marriage was *valid:* i.e., they had a good Catholic marriage for many years, but it died. Dramatic personality changes in mid-life, some personal tragedy which seemed to destroy the husband-wife relationship, another person who wins away a spouse—all have led to destroy a marriage and to divorce.

It is very important to indicate from a pastoral point of view that numerous persons in this "second category" cannot apply for an annulment for "internal reasons": i.e., since they are convinced that the first marriage was truly a valid and good one, although now ended, it is impossible for them *in conscience* to seek the possibility of an annulment, which would be a statement in the external forum that there was never a bond there in the first place.

We saw in Chapter Four that some authors present certain criteria for eucharistic participation for those who sustain a "good conscience" regarding their first marriage. Some authors narrow these reasons to apply only to those persons who perceive their first marriage to be invalid, while others extend the possibility of eucharistic participation to those who perceive their first marriage to be either valid or invalid.

Because of this obvious confusion in the vocabulary between "good faith" and "good conscience," it is essential to study carefully the way the Church authentically understands the meaning of "good faith." It might be helpful to repeat here, however, that in the eyes of the Church a person living in an irregular second marriage may not receive the Eucharist because of the contradiction that this present union sustains in regard to the first bond of marriage. Chapter Four explained the theology behind this "countersign," and now we must carefully further this discussion by scrutinizing the nuances within the Church's teaching regarding the internal forum and good faith.

Congregation for the Doctrine of the Faith

On 11 April 1973, the Congregation for the Doctrine of the Faith issued a statement regarding the administration of the Sacraments to those in irregular unions. Because of its importance, we will cite here the entire document:

> This Sacred Congregation, whose duty it is to safeguard the teaching of faith and morals throughout the Catholic world, has taken careful note of the spread of new opinions which either deny or attempt to call into doubt the teaching of the magisterium of the Church on the indissolubility of matrimony.

Opinions of this kind have not only been published in Catholic books and periodicals, but have also begun to appear in seminaries, Catholic schools and even in the ecclesiastical tribunals of some dioceses.

The opinions, moreover, have been joined to other doctrinal or pastoral reasons to form an argument for justifying abuses against current discipline on the admission to the sacraments of those who are living in irregular unions.

Consequently, this Sacred Congregation in its plenary meeting of 1972 examined the matter and now has the mandate, approved by the Supreme Pontiff, to strongly urge upon Your Excellency diligent vigilance, so that all those assigned to teach religion in schools of any level or in various institutes, or who function as "officialis" in ecclesiastical tribunals, will remain faithful to the teaching of the Church regarding the indissolubility of marriage and will reduce this to practical effect in the tribunals.

In regard to admission to the sacraments, the ordinaries are asked on the one hand to stress observance of current discipline and, on the other hand, to take care that the pastors of souls exercise special care to seek out those who are living in an irregular union by applying to the solution of such cases, in addition to other right means, the Church's approved practice in the internal forum.

Theological Analysis

This document of the CDF, under the signature of its former prefect, Cardinal Franjo Seper, urges diocesan bishops to pastorally seek out those who are living in irregular unions and investigate the possibility of an ecclesiastical annulment. As we have already seen in Chapter One, this same point is urged by Pope John Paul II in his 1981 exhortation *Familiaris Consortio,* nos. 79–84.

At the same time, however, this 1973 document from the CDF likewise urges diocesan bishops to use "in addition . . . the Church's approved practice in the internal forum."

As we have noted already in this chapter, jurisdiction in the internal forum always looks to the spiritual good of one of the faithful. The internal forum is appealed to because of the presence of some conflict between the conscience of a person and the external law of the Church.

The Church's approved practice in the internal forum is properly administered when it is prudently determined that one of the faithful truly possesses "good faith" concerning the matter at hand. In addition to the discussion we have already had, the counsel of the traditional moralist Father Noldin is instructive:

> *Even when the penitent is judged open to acting on advice, but the advice would cause harm to a third party, for example, harm to children if an invalid marriage were broken up, the advice or admonition should be omitted. If there is doubt whether the admonition will be harmful or helpful it should be omitted. . . . But the individual must be instructed, even in the case where no good is foreseen to result from informing him or her, in the case where public scandal is involved.*[3]

What is an example of "good faith" where the internal forum of the Church might be properly employed?

In 1975, Mary marries Harry and they attain a civil

divorce in 1980. In 1982 Mary brings her 1975 marriage to Harry to an ecclesiastical tribunal for the possibility of an annulment on the grounds of an intention against children *(contra bonum prolis)*. Mary "knows" that Harry would not have children but she cannot prove this fact in law to the tribunal. The tribunal could not accept this case for reasons of lack of proof.

In 1983, Mary marries Bill in a civil ceremony, still absolutely convinced in "good faith" that her 1975 marriage to Harry was invalid on recognized canonical grounds.

Mary and Bill are living in a parish where virtually no one knows about Mary's previous marriage to Harry. Convinced as she is of the invalidity of her first marriage, she regularly participates in the Eucharist. Why? Because (a) she truly believes that her first marriage was invalid, and (b) she deeply believes that she has committed no sin in marrying Bill or in participating in the Eucharist.

Assuming that scandal is avoided, the Church's "approved practice in the internal forum" can properly be used in this case and Mary may, in good conscience continue to participate in the Eucharist.

This example might serve as a good critique regarding the two meanings given above regarding "good conscience." In light of the distinction previously made regarding good conscience (i.e., those in good conscience who believe their first marriage to be invalid, and those who believe their first marriage to be valid), the Church's "approved practice in the internal forum" cannot be used properly in a situation where a person truly believes that their first marriage was valid. In addition, the internal forum solution can be used properly for those who believe that their first marriage was invalid *only* if certain criteria are present:

First, the person involved is truly convinced of the invalidity of the first union.

Second, that person has applied for an annulment for this first marriage, with grounds recognized in canonical jurisprudence (i.e., he or she simply cannot maintain that the marriage "died").

Third, that person has entered the second union not only believing the invalidity of the first bond, but truly sensing that they are committing no sin in entering into this new marriage, because of the "good faith" regarding their first marital union.

In light of these criteria, it is quite apparent that the internal forum solution can only be properly used when the remarried couple is truly convinced that the first marriage is invalid. The pastoral problem becomes extremely complex if a couple truly believe that the first marriage was valid, but also truly believe that this fact does not matter in terms of their freedom to receive the Eucharist. In light of the counsel given above by Father Noldin, traditional moral advice instructs Church ministers that "if there is doubt whether the admonition will be harmful or helpful it should be omitted. . . . "

At the same time, however, Fr. Noldin points out that scandal must always be avoided. What is clear, then, is that the teaching of the Church on the invalidity of second marriages after valid first marriages is eminently clear, and one could not possibly doubt this teaching and be in "good faith." Respecting the advice of Fr. Noldin, then, the pastoral minister must be extremely sensitive to those persons in an invalid second marriage and the proper use of the internal forum solution.

Summary

Doubtlessly, questions concerning the internal forum and good faith are very complex, and the Church's teaching about the subject is quite specific and nuanced. It is thus important to correctly use the internal forum solution in the Church, and to properly appreciate the authentic meaning of "good faith" (it does seem at times that the concept of "good conscience" takes on a much broader meaning than the approved concept of "good faith").[4]

What conclusions might we draw from this discussion?

First, the internal forum solution does exist in the Church, but this "solution" has a specific meaning, closely related to "good faith."

Second, it is really not pastorally viable to so accentuate an individual's personal sincerity at the price of an individual's irregularity: i.e., all decisions made in the internal forum must properly discern the possible effects of this decision in the external forum, as obviously the person will continue to live within the communion of the faithful.

Third, in light of present canonical jurisprudence as well as the document of the CDF of 1973 and the subsequent letter of Archbishop Hamer to Archbishop Bernardin of March 21, 1975, the internal forum may properly be used under these circumstances:

1. A sanation *(sanatio in radice):* a common example here would concern a mixed religion marriage, when the non-Catholic person refuses to come to the Church to have the marriage validated ("blessed"), claiming that he or she was married once (civilly) and thus has no intention of going before a Catholic deacon or priest to renew this contract.

In such a case, for the sake of the faith of the Catholic party, the Church heals (sanates) this marriage by dispensing the couple from proper form (i.e., a Catholic is bound to marry before the proper pastor and two witnesses).

The Catholic party is then free to participate in the sacraments.

2. Pope John Paul II in *Familiaris Consortio* (1982) indicated that should a couple be living in an irregular marriage and believe their first marriage to be valid, and they are unable now to separate for pastoral reasons (e.g., care for children), they

may participate in the sacraments if they are willing to live a life of continence.

3. In a case where a person or couple are truly unaware of the invalidity of their present union: we noted the example of the Jewish person who was previously married and divorced and truly believed that the previous union was no union at all in the eyes of the Catholic Church.

4. In the case where a couple have attempted to attain an annulment but to no avail: these people truly believe that the first union (e.g., of one of them) was invalid *and* the reasons for the invalidity have foundation in the Church's law. In addition, they truly believe that this present union is the true one.

It should be clear, then, in this case, that the *sine qua non* of the internal forum solution is the objective invalidity of a previous marriage for reasons that are recognized in Church law *and* truly existing in fact, but the establishing of the fact is not possible for an external forum declaration of nullity.

The point here, then, is that subjective reasons for alleging invalidity (e.g., the first marriage is dead because it is irretrievably lost), no matter how sincerely held, have no place in the proper use of the internal forum solution. The key factor, therefore, is the "informed conscience" of the person, judging with moral certitude that he or she is free to marry because of the *de facto* invalidity of the previous marriage.

In this entire question, the words of Pope John Paul II in *Familiaris Consortio* are vital:

> *I earnestly call upon pastors in the whole community of the faithful to help the divorced and with solicitous care to make certain that they do not consider themselves as separated from the Church, for as baptized persons they can and, indeed, must share in its life.*[5]

6

The Question of Excommunication

The Third Council of Baltimore (1884)

In a *History of the Councils of Baltimore (1791–1884)*, Peter Guilday writes:

> . . . the *"enormous scandal" of divorce was exposed, for the bishops "were determined to employ the severest authority of the Church" against any of the faithful "guilty of so heinous a crime and to cut them off from her communion."*[1]

The "enormous scandal" of divorce had been recognized by the American bishops since 1843 at the Fifth Provincial Council of Baltimore.[2] Since 1843, the American bishops sustained a great fear that the growing divorce mentality among Catholics would de facto equal apostasy.

In the United States of the nineteenth century, a hostile atmosphere surrounded the relationship between the established Protestant churches and the immigrant Catholic Church. When a Catholic left a spouse, and with full knowledge that he or she must not remarry, and then married illegally and in a Protestant church, this marriage was considered a "double" abandonment: deserting the spouse and often children, and deserting one's Catholicism. In this historical context, then, it is not surprising that the American bishops were so severe in their legislation on the matter of divorce and remarriage.

The seriousness with which the bishops regarded marriage can be seen in the pastoral letter of the Third Council of Baltimore:

> *The security of the Christian home is in the indissolubility of the marriage tie. Christian marriage, once consummated, can never be dissolved save by death. Let it be well understood that even adultery, though it may justify "separation from bed and board," cannot loose the marriage tie, so that either of the parties may marry again during the life of the other. Nor has "legal divorce" the slightest power, before God, to loose the bond of marriage and to make a subsequent marriage valid. "Whom God has joined together, let not man put asunder." In common with all Christian believers and friends of civilization, we deplore the havoc wrought by the divorce-laws of our country. These laws are fast loosening the foundations of society. Let Catholics at least remember that such divorces are powerless in conscience. Let them enter into marriage only through worthy and holy motives, and with the blessings of religion, especially with the blessing of the Nuptial Mass. And then, far from wishing for means of escape from their union, they will rejoice that it cannot be divided but by death.[3]*

In 1884, the Third Plenary Council of Baltimore thus promulgated this statute:

> *It is clearly evident that they are guilty of the gravest fault who petition the civil authority for a dissolution of marriage, or even worse, having obtained a civil divorce and without regard for the lawful bond, which in the sight of God and the Church still endures, attempt to enter another marriage. In order*

*to curb such crimes, we enact the penalty of excom-
munication to be incurred automatically by those
who, after obtaining a divorce, dare to attempt civil
marriage.*[4]

Classical commentators on the old Code of Canon Law
consistently made reference to this statute no. 124 of Baltimore
III:[5] for example,

*Poenam excommunicationis statuimus ordinario
reservatam, ipso facto incurrendam ab eis qui,
postquam divortium civile obtinuerint, matrimonium
ausi fuerint attentare.*

The key phrase in this statute is *"matrimonium ausi fuerint attentare"* (dare to attempt marriage). We must carefully
study this point of the statute.

Canonical Interpretation

Bouscaren, Ellis and Korth in their *Commentary* on the
old Code of Canon Law make the following important
interpretation:

If the law contains the following words: praesump-
serit, ausus fuerit, scienter, studiose, temerarie, con-
sulto agerit, *or others similar to them which require
full knowledge and deliberation, any diminution of
imputability on the part of either the intellect or the
will exempts [the delinquent] from penalties imposed
by anticipatory sentence [latae sententiae].*[6]

The new Code of Canon Law (1983) affirms the same
point being made here by these classical canonical interpreters.
Canon 1323 points out that persons are not liable to a penalty

if there was inadvertence or error on their part, or if they acted under compulsion or grave fear.[7] The proper understanding of the Third Council of Baltimore's use of the term *"ausi fuerint"* (dare) is captured well by L. C. Farley:

> It should be noted that the Council [*Baltimore III*] employed the term ausi fuerint *("those who dare . . . ").* Hence any diminution of imputability, either on the part of the intellect or of the will, exempts such persons from the censure, according to canon 2229:2. It can be and is argued that such a reduction of imputability, however small, is always present in such second marriages, since they are entered into to secure civil benefits and approbation of the second union, and not simply to fly in the face of Church authority. Furthermore, the element of contumacy is necessary according to canon 2242:1, in order to incur the censure. According to canon 2242:2, in order to incur an ipso facto censure, it is sufficient that the law be transgressed, unless the guilty party has a legitimate excuse to do this. When one takes into account the civil benefits involved, particularly an honorable estate for the children, the civil marriage is hardly contracted by those who ausi fuerint.[8]

A final canonical point is important before reaching a conclusion about this entire matter. In the new Code, the following canon is important:

> Laws which prescribe a penalty, or restrict the free exercise of rights, or contain an exception to the law, are to be interpreted strictly (c. 18; c. 19 in the old Code).

Since the Third Council of Baltimore issued a statute which prohibited divorce *and* remarriage under the automatic penalty of excommunication, such a penalty must be interpreted "strictly": i.e., the penalty applies only to those persons who strictly/specifically transgress the prohibited action. In light of this legislation, a person "daring" to remarry would be a Catholic whose motivation in remarrying sustains a basic disregard for the prohibition of the Church and marries only or basically for this reason.

On the contrary, as we have seen, if there is any "diminution of imputability" in the person's intellect or will, then the *penalty* is not incurred. This does not make divorce and remarriage permissible or "all right," but it does indicate that not every Catholic coming under the legislation of Baltimore III incurred the penalty of excommunication, since, as Farley indicated, the motivation for remarriage was certainly other than a "daring" reason.

It is historically understandable that the bishops wanted to curb the growing rise of divorce and remarriage among American Catholics, especially in light of the historical context of the time. As the Church continued its growth, however, it became more and more apparent that Catholics who de facto divorced and remarried did not do so out of a disregard for Church law, but rather for other motivations: for example, falling in love with a new spouse; a desire to give familial protection to children. It was this growing pastoral sensitivity which later in 1977 led the American bishops to request the Holy See to drop this penalty of excommunication.

One final point must be mentioned. The Third Council of Baltimore promulgated the penalty of excommunication only in regard to those Catholics who divorced *and* remarried. For many years in this country numerous Catholics have misunderstood this legislation. For example, there are some Catholics to this day who believe that "the Church" teaches that a

Catholic who merely divorces is excommunicated. It is thus pastorally essential to underline the fact that Baltimore III never maintained such a position.

Statement of the American Bishops (1977)

With approval from Rome, the American bishops in May 1977 voted to drop the penalty of excommunication for all Catholics who divorced and remarried. The Chair of the Bishops' Committee on Canonical Affairs, Bishop Cletus O'Donnell, issued a statement explaining this decision. The statement itself deserves study; but we will here quote only major factors regarding the question of excommunication:

We wish to help divorced and remarried Catholics without seeming to weaken the unbreakable bond of marriage covenant entered into freely in Christ. The decision of the Catholic bishops of the United States to seek to remove one burden from the shoulders of divorced and remarried Catholics—the Church penalty of excommunication—must therefore be prefaced by a clear explanation.

Excommunication is the most severe of Church penalties. It means separation from the community of the faithful, prohibition of reception of sacraments, loss of any share in the public prayers of the Church, prohibition of the holding of Church offices and the exercise of Church jurisdiction, etc. . . .

After study and reflection, the bishops of the United States have concluded that the removal of this particular excommunication . . . can foster healing and rec-

onciliation for many Catholics remarried after divorce.

The positive dimensions of this decision are very real. It welcomes back to the community of believers in Christ all who may have been separated by excommunication. . . . Perhaps above all, it is a gesture of love and reconciliation from the other members of the Church.

However, this important step is not a total solution to the problems of these people. . . . The Church cannot recognize as valid and sacramental those second marriages after divorce, unless there has been a determination by a Church tribunal on behalf of the Church community that the persons involved are free to marry in Christ the Lord. . . . And the lifting of the burden of excommunication does not of itself permit those who have remarried after divorce to receive the sacraments of penance and the Holy Eucharist. This last and most difficult question—return to full eucharistic communion—can be resolved only in a limited number of instances, depending on the particular circumstances.

This decision . . . is only a single step, but it offers encouragement and hope to disaffected or alienated Catholics. . . . For the future, thorough preparation for marriage and support for marriage and family life by the whole community of the Church are the only genuine solutions.

It is clear in this statement that the repeal of the penalty of excommunication does not alter anything regarding the

Church's attitude about the invalidity of second marriages of Catholics who have not attained a Church annulment of a prior bond. At the same time, however, the repeal does mean several important things:

First, that most Catholics in this part of the century who accept a civil divorce and then remarry do not include in their motives a desire to leave the Catholic Church.

Second, that the Church truly desires to encourage such people to make use of devotional, spiritual, charitable and pastoral activities of the Church that are permitted to them.

Summary

The question of excommunication has been a significant canonical and pastoral difficulty for American Catholics. It is very important to appreciate the specific understanding of excommunication as promulgated by Baltimore III, in light of canonical jurisprudence.

We have seen that the number of Catholics who de facto remarried "daringly" were probably minimal, and this factor doubtlessly led the American bishops in 1977 to request Rome to drop the penalty of excommunication. While the repeal of this penalty sustains numerous positive benefits, the "last and most difficult question," as Bishop O'Donnell pointed out, of eucharistic participation still remains.

The lifting of the penalty of excommunication is certainly a recognition that the vast majority of Catholics who divorce and remarry do not include in this decision nor in their motives a hatred for the Church or a desire to leave the Church. This fact was clearly born out in the various statistics which we studied in Chapter One. Furthermore, in many cases, Catholics enter second marriages with seriousness, fidelity, stability and a deep realization of obligations and responsibilities to a former spouse.

7

Scriptural Data

The Context

The scriptural materials regarding divorce and remarriage are of utmost importance in this whole discussion. The pivotal points which arise from the scriptural data sustain at least these questions: (a) Since St. Matthew and St. Paul seemed to have taken the absolute prohibition of Jesus concerning divorce in such a way that an "exception" to this prohibition was possible, is it further possible to make other accommodations in our own day? (b) Are the scriptural prohibitions regarding divorce understood within the Bible as absolute or as a moral ideal? Such questions as these are obviously central to the scriptural materials, and we will address them as clearly as possible in this chapter.

In order to appreciate the complexity of the question, it is important to see precisely how certain authors frame the problem. Joseph A. Fitzmyer, S. J. gives one clear example:

> If Matthew under inspiration could have been moved to add an exceptive phrase to the saying of Jesus about divorce that he found in an absolute form in either his Marcan source or in 'Q', or if Paul likewise under inspiration could introduce into his writing an exception on his own authority, then why cannot the Spirit-guided institutional Church of a later generation make a similar exception in view of problems confronting Christian married life of its day or so-

*called broken marriages (not really envisioned in the
New Testament) as it has done in some situations?*[1]

Scriptural exegetes see the need to carefully discern the
process by which the teaching of Jesus was remembered, com-
municated, interpreted and adapted in the practice of the early
Christian communities. Father Bruce Vawter furthers this
discussion:

> *The Christian communities which have accepted
> divorce as a deplorable but an inevitable fact of life
> have taken some guidance admittedly from New Tes-
> tament exegesis, but far more they have taken their
> guidance from other indices to the realities of the
> human condition in their times, and this is perhaps
> partly as it should be.*[2]

A final quotation helps contextualize the state of the
question:

> *There is another possibility which ought to be con-
> sidered, namely, that Jesus established a moral ideal,
> a counsel without constituting it a legal norm. In con-
> nection with the Beatitudes he spoke also of divorce
> (Mt 5:27–32). One must therefore inquire if this is
> to be understood literally as a command or merely as
> a moral ideal.*[3]

It is concerning these questions of "accommodation" and
"moral ideal" that we turn to in this chapter, as well as in
Chapter Eight.

The Texts: Old Testament

There are two major Old Testament texts which are important to this discussion. The first text is Genesis 1:27–28:

> So God created man in his own image, in the image of God he created him; male and female he created them. And God blessed them, and God said to them, "Be fruitful and multiply, and fill the earth and subdue it; and have dominion over the fish of the sea and the birds of the air and over every living thing that moves upon the earth."

This text from the first chapter of Genesis dates from the sixth century and demonstrates that God has made men and women in his own image and that he is the author of the total human unity of man and woman. In addition, the text indicates, one of the responsibilities given to the "male and female" is procreation.

The other Old Testament text that is important for our discussion as we look into the New Testament texts is Genesis 2:22–24:

> . . . and the rib which the Lord God had taken from the man he made into a woman and brought her to the man. Then the man said, "This at last is bone of my bones and flesh of my flesh; she shall be called woman, because she was taken out of man."

> Therefore, a man leaves his father and his mother and cleaves to his wife, and they become one flesh.

This text from Genesis 2 dates from the tenth century and it is a text that stresses the "one flesh" *(una vita)* unity that the husband and wife create. As we shall see, St. Paul will refer back to this text from Genesis 2.

The Texts: New Testament

The New Testament contains five texts that are important to our discussion. First, Mark 10:2–12:

> *And Pharisees came up and in order to test him asked, "Is it lawful for a man to divorce his wife?" He answered them, "What did Moses command you?" They said, "Moses allowed a man to write a certificate of divorce, and to put her away." But Jesus said to them, "For your hardness of heart he wrote you this commandment. But from the beginning of creation, 'God made them male and female.' 'For this reason a man shall leave his father and mother and be joined to his wife, and the two shall become one.' So they are no longer two but one. What therefore God has joined together, let not man put asunder."*

> *And in the house the disciples asked him again about this matter. And he said to them, "Whoever divorces his wife and marries another, commits adultery against her; and if she divorces her husband and marries another, she commits adultery."*

Clearly in St. Mark Jesus notes that divorce was never allowed "from the beginning" because of the unity (the *una vita*) of the husband/wife relationship. It is additionally important to note that St. Mark makes reference to prohibitions of divorce for both the husband *and* the wife.

The text of St. Mark refers to the law of Moses, as expressed in Deuteronomy 24:1–4:

When a man takes a wife and marries her, if then she finds no favor in his eyes because he has found some indecency in her, and he writes her a bill of divorce and puts it in her hand and sends her out of his house, and she departs out of his house, and if she goes and becomes another man's wife, and the latter husband dislikes her and writes her a bill of divorce and puts it in her hand and sends her out of his house, or if the latter husband dies, who took her to be his wife, then her former husband, who sent her away, may not take her again to be his wife, after she has been defiled; for that is an abomination before the Lord, and you shall not bring guilt upon the land which the Lord your God gives you for an inheritance.

Mark 10:2–12 is a composite saying, the first part addressed to the Pharisees and the second part a dominical ("And in the house . . . ") saying addressed later to the disciples in a house. Verse 9 brings God into the picture and clearly formulates Jesus' prohibition of divorce in absolute terms. The phrase in v. 11 ("against her") is almost certainly a Marcan addition which makes Jesus' words express the fact that adultery against a woman is a reality now to be considered.

Second, Luke 16:18:

Everyone who divorces his wife and marries another commits adultery, and he who marries a woman divorced from her husband commits adultery.

We find here in Luke an absolute prohibition of divorce, found also within a dominical saying. This prohibition is in the

form of a declaratory legal statement, a judgment about a husband's marriage after divorce: it is adultery. In addition, Luke
here writes about the subsequent marriage being that of the
man; the text is thus written in the context of the wife as the
chattel of the husband. What is new here, however, is the
branding of the man's action as adulterous.

Third, Matthew 5:31–32:

> *It was also said, "Whoever divorces his wife, let him
> give her a certificate of divorce." But I say to you that
> everyone who divorces his wife, except on the
> ground of unchastity, makes her an adulteress; and
> whoever marries a divorced woman commits
> adultery.*

This text appears as part of the Sermon on the Mount and
it is here that Matthew "adds" his exceptive phrase, " . . .
except on the ground of unchastity . . . " *(parektos logou porneias)*. The Matthew text, however, does not add what Luke
has said, " . . . and marrying another . . . " *(kai gamon heteran)*.
In this text, Matthew relates divorce itself to adultery, and not
divorce and subsequent marriage. Thus divorce *itself* is, in
Matthew's eyes, the cause of adultery.

Fourth, Matthew 19:3–12:

> *And Pharisees came up to him and tested him by ask-
> ing, "Is it lawful to divorce one's wife for any
> cause?" He answered, "Have you not read that he
> who made them from the beginning made them male
> and female, and said, 'For this reason a man shall
> leave his father and mother and be joined to his wife,
> and the two shall become one'? So they are no longer
> two but one. What therefore God has joined
> together, let no man put asunder." They said to him,*

*"Why then did Moses command one to give a certif-
icate of divorce, and to put her away?" He said to
them, "For your hardness of heart Moses allowed
you to divorce your wives, but from the beginning it
was not so. And I say to you: whoever divorces his
wife, except for unchastity, and marries another,
commits adultery; and he who marries a divorced
woman commits adultery."*

*The disciples said to him, "If such is the case of a
man with his wife, it is not expedient to marry." But
he said to them, "Not all men can receive this precept, but only those to whom it is given. . . . "*

This text is derived from the Marcan source, but modified
to suit Jewish-Christian concerns, as we shall soon see. In
other words, it is cast in terms of the Hillel-Shammai dispute
and as with Mark we have here a composite. Minus the exceptive clause, this prohibition is derived from Mark 10 and
adapted by Matthew for the sake of Christians living in a
mixed community. We will soon discuss the implications of
this adaptation.

Fifth, 1 Corinthians 7:10–11 and 12–14:

*To the married I give charge, not I but the Lord, that
the wife should not separate from her husband (but if
she does, let her remain single or else be reconciled
to her husband)—and that the husband should not
divorce his wife.*

*To the rest I say, not the Lord, that if any brother has
a wife who is an unbeliever, and she consents to live
with him, he should not divorce her. If any woman
has a husband who is an unbeliever, and he consents*

to live with her, she should not divorce him. For the unbelieving husband is consecrated through his wife, and the unbelieving wife is consecrated through her husband. Otherwise, your children would be unclean, but as it is they are holy.

This text dates to about 56 A.D. and thus is the earliest attestation recorded regarding the divorce prohibition as traced to Jesus. In this text, St. Paul attributes the prohibition to "the Lord," thus investing the prohibition with the authority of the risen Christ. It is an absolute prohibition: neither husband nor wife can divorce. If the woman should be divorced, she should remain "unmarried" or be reconciled. Marriage, then, after divorce is prohibited by Paul. Paul is thus realizing that divorce does take place, and this is a clear contrast to what appears in verses 12–15 that a "believing woman" is not bound if an unbelieving husband separates from her.

It is clear thus far that four writers in the New Testament record the divorce prohibition as traced to Jesus: 1 Corinthians 7:10–11; Mark 10:2–12; Luke 16:18; Matthew 5:31–32 and 19:3–9.

Textual Interpretation

Clearly, the scriptural materials regarding divorce and remarriage are quite complex, especially in regard to the absolute prohibition of divorce by Jesus and the adaptation of this prohibition by St. Matthew and St. Paul. The exegesis of these texts is beyond the scope of this chapter, but it is important to understand at least briefly some of the major points about the adaptations, since they so intimately affect both a theological and pastoral appreciation of contemporary questions regarding divorce and remarriage.[4]

First, it is important to look carefully at the "exceptive clauses" in Matthew 5:32 and Matthew 19:9. The major question is whether these exceptive clauses de facto limit Jesus' absolute prohibition?

We have already cited Deuteronomy 24:1–4. This text assumes the institution of divorce, but it also regulates the institution: i.e., it protects the woman by stipulating a written bill of divorce; she can then remarry and not be stigmatized as an adulteress. The problem becomes more complex as we recall that in Paul, Mark and Luke Jesus rescinds this whole law as well as the whole institution of divorce as legitimated by the Torah.

In order to properly understand and appreciate the Matthean exceptive clauses, it is necessary to remind ourselves of the dispute between the rabbinic schools of Hillel and Shammai regarding the ambiguous phrase in Deuteronomy 24:1. This verse names the grounds for divorce as *ĕrwat dābār* (the shame of a thing, or a shameful thing).

The school of Hillel stressed the *dābār* (thing) and concluded that practically "anything" constituted grounds for divorce: e.g., displeasure at the woman's cooking; finding a prettier woman. On the other hand, the school of Shammai stressed the *ĕrwat* (shame) and concluded that the reason for divorce had to be serious: i.e., something that involved shame. An example would be adultery. The school of Shammai actually would invert Deuteronomy 24:1 to read *debār ĕrwâ* (a thing of shame).

The question thus arises in the exceptive clauses of Matthew whether he is siding with the school of Shammai by inserting the prohibition *parektos logou porneias* (except on the ground of impurity). The Greek phrase *logou porneias* literally means "a word of impurity," a close translation of the Hebrew *debār ĕrwa* (a word of shame). It thus seems that Matthew (or his church) is siding with this meaning in Shammai.

For the school of Shammai, the grounds for divorce should not be understood, however, only as adultery, as other

immodest conduct short of adultery might well have come
under the rubric of shame. In addition, it seems unlikely that
Matthew alone would introduce such a major change, and thus
too the "exceptive clauses" probably represent the tradition of
Matthew's church.

An additional problem in this textual analysis regards the
role of Jesus himself: i.e., was Jesus caught in this dispute
between Hillel and Shammai? It is strange that *logou porneias*
occurs *not* in Matthew 19:9 where Jesus is supposedly being
asked to choose between the two interpretations; but rather in
Matthew 5:31–32, where no such clear-cut choice is indicated.
Meier in *Christ, Church and Morality in the First Gospel* thus
concludes that *parektos logou porneias* does not have to be taken
as a literal translation of *debār érwa*. It makes perfectly good
sense in ordinary Greek as "except on the grounds of impurity." In fact, the Greek Septuagint translation renders the
Hebrew as *askēmon pragma* (a shameful thing). It is thus not all
that certain whether Jesus in fact was caught in the debate
between these two schools.

Second, in general the meaning of *porneia* means "any
illicit sexual activity." If *porneia* refers to Shammai interpretations, it must receive a wide meaning: i.e., impure sexual
activity *and* social immodesty. As Meier indicates, however,
such a translation seems strange in Matthew's radicalizing
Jesus. If Jesus is being stricter than Shammai by restricting the
grounds for divorce to adultery alone, we run into another
problem with *porneia*: it has a wide range of meaning in Greek.
Yet, in the New Testament, adultery is rendered by various
forms of the verb *moicheuō*. *Porneia* is sometimes used to refer
to married people, but always in a given context: e.g., prosti-
tution, religious infidelity. Matthew, then, clearly employs
words such as *moicheia* when he wants to refer to adultery.

The conclusion is that if Matthew wished to name adultery as a grounds for divorce, he would have been forced to

use some form of the word *moicheia* (see, e.g., Mt 5:19, where both words are used). Therefore, whatever *porneia* means, it does *not* mean adultery.

Third, we are told that the Pharisees came to Jesus "testing" him: i.e., they had a malicious intent. If they were merely asking Jesus whether he favors Hillel or Shammai, the verb *peirazontes* (testing) would never have been used. After all, both schools were respectable.

Fourth, how might we properly interpret *porneia?* We know that in the first century B.C. and A.D., the Jewish people were almost unique in their strict condemnation of incestuous marriages, as prohibited in Leviticus 18:6–186:

> *None of you shall approach anyone near of kin to him to uncover nakedness. . . . You shall not uncover the nakedness of your father, which is the nakedness of your mother; she is your mother, you shall not uncover her nakedness. . . . You shall not uncover the nakedness of your sister. . . . You shall not uncover the nakedness of your son's daughter or of your daughter's daughter . . . it is wickedness. And you shall not take a woman as a rival wife to her sister, uncovering her nakedness while her sister is yet alive.*

These prohibitions were so strict in Jewish law and custom that if a Gentile had entered one of these marriages in "good faith," and now converted to Judaism, the question arose of whether or not it was necessary for this person to dismiss his wife.

Matthew's church replied that an incestuous marriage contracted before a convert's baptism was not to be condoned because it is not a true union, being forbidden by Leviticus. It was null and void from the beginning and thus did not fall under Jesus' prohibition of divorce which was concerned with "genuine marriages."

In addition, two other texts in the New Testament clearly use *porneia* to refer to incestuous marriages: Acts 15:29 and 1 Corinthians 5:1. Clearly, then, *porneia* refers in Matthew's church not to adultery but rather to the prohibition of incestuous marriages forbidden by Leviticus. This interpretation of *porneia* is the preferred one, and the Qumran evidence also supports this interpretation (i.e., the Damascus Document).

Fifth, Matthew seems to have "added" the exceptive clause because he was seeking to resolve a problem in early Jewish-Christian communities and to deal pastorally with the situation of Gentiles who were coming into Christianity and already found themselves in marital conditions proscribed for Jewish people by Leviticus 18.

Summary

As is evident in Mark 10:9, Matthew 19:6 and Luke 16:18, Jesus himself taught an absolute and unqualified prohibition of divorce. The "additional" material that we have seen in Mark 10:12, Matthew 5:32 and 19:9 and 1 Corinthians 7:10 are developments best explained in terms of the contexts in which the prohibitions were repeated.

The Matthean exceptive phrases clearly do not make adultery a basis for divorce, as we have demonstrated.

At the same time, however, the critical pastoral question arises that if exceptions were made in the primitive churches, is it not possible for the Spirit-guided Church of today to make other "exceptions" in light of contemporary problems facing the Church?

This certainly remains a very difficult and sensitive question, one which the Church continues to search and struggle with.

A final word should be had here concerning the text of Paul in 1 Corinthians 7:10–11 and 12–14. This text dates from about 56 A.D. and thus carries tremendous import as an obviously primitive scriptural text. Verse 12 is addressed to "the rest," which means, in our terminology, mixed marriages, as Paul would be referring to two Christians in verse 10. Mixed marriages in this sense would mean a Christian and a non-Christian.

Paul makes clear that it is *his* teaching and not the Lord's that in *all* marriages peace must always be the goal and that one's religious beliefs are essential for achieving this goal. It is thus important to note that Paul strongly believes that the very presence of the Christian is a source of consecration for the non-believer. This is why, in this text, the Christian may not initiate a separation.

The Pauline privilege of canonical jurisprudence is certainly an outgrowth of this teaching in 1 Corinthians 7, although canonically the law is now very distant from St. Paul's original meaning. Consequently, we should not lose sight of the fact that Paul is stressing that in every marriage peace must be the mutual goal of the couple and that one's religious beliefs are quite essential to achieving this goal.

In this light, the statistical data gathered by Preister is quite extraordinary:

> *Daily prayer by both spouses has an extraordinarily powerful relationship with sexual fulfillment. Those marriages in which both spouses pray every day are almost twice as likely to be marriages in which both spouses say their sexual fulfillment is excellent.*[5]

8

Divorce in History

Overview

The scriptural materials which we have studied have remained the bedrock and framework for the Church's historical inquiries into the meaning of divorce and remarriage down through the ages. For example, Karl Lehmann writes:

> ... they [*Paul and Matthew*] *were always aware of the contradiction to Scripture and saw in this action the possibility of avoiding even greater evils (in other words, they applied the principle of the lesser evil).*[1]

Lehmann is indicating here that in the scriptural evidence there is an absolute precept against divorce, and this precept should not be interpreted as an "ideal" or "goal."[2] At the same time, however, Lehmann acknowledges that both Paul and the Matthean church made certain concessions to this absolute precept. As we shall soon see, this same "duality" is found in the history of this question. As Richard A. McCormick, S.J. thus remarks: "The tension between the precept of indissolubility and human failure always remained."[3]

In a comprehensive study of divorce laws between the time of Constantine (331 A.D.) and Justinian (535 A.D.), John T. Noonan concludes:

> *The calm acceptance of dissolubility by the law shows at this time, between 331 and 566, no defini-*

tive Christian position had been established on remarriage and divorce.[4]

This lack of a definitive Christian position centered largely around the interpretation of the Matthean exceptive phrase in Matthew 5:32, *parektos logou porneias* (except in the matter of *porneia*). Origin, Lactantius, Basil the Great, Ambrosiaster, Asterius of Amasea, Epiphanius of Salamis, Victor of Antioch, Avitus of Vienna, and the Councils of Areles (314), Milvis (416), Vannes (461), and Adge (506) all upheld the right of the husband to divorce an adulterous wife. In addition, Origen and Basil the Great upheld the right of an "innocent" wife to remarry who was maliciously deserted by her husband.[5]

During the twelfth century debate continued between the school of Bologna and the school of Paris. The school of Bologna maintained that carnal relations were necessary to form the matrimonial bond, whereas the school of Paris taught that mutual consent forms the marriage contract. This debate continued until the proclamation of Pope Alexander III (1159–1181) which taught that marriage is constituted by mutual consent and that consummation adds a perfection to this consent and makes it a complete union. This long debate and papal pronouncement were all brought together for continued discussion and resolution at the Council of Trent.

The Council of Trent: 24th Session (1563)

The Council of Trent dealt with the doctrine of the sacrament of matrimony in its 24th session in 1563 (DS1797–1812). The Council of Trent included many teachings in its doctrine about matrimony, but the major teaching which we desire to study here is Trent's Canon 7:

> *If anyone shall say that the Church errs in that it taught and teaches that in accordance with evangeli-*

> *cal and apostolic doctrine (Mt 19:6ff; Mk 10:6ff; 1*
> *Cor 7:10ff) the bond of matrimony cannot be dis-*
> *solved by reason of adultery on the part of one of the*
> *parties, and that both, or even the innocent party who*
> *gave no reason for adultery, cannot contract another*
> *marriage during the lifetime of the other, and that he*
> *is guilty of adultery who, having put away the adul-*
> *teress, shall marry another, and she also who, having*
> *put away the adulterer, shall marry another—anath-*
> *ema sit (DS1807).*

Because of the significance of Canon 7, it is important to see its Latin phrasing:

> Si quis dixeret Ecclesiam errare cum docuit et docet, iuxta evangelicam et apostolicam doctrinam.

> Propter adulterium alterius coniugum matrimonii vinculum non posse dissolvi.

> Et utrumque coniugum, vel saltem innocentem, qui causam adulterii non dedit, non posse, altero coniuge vivente, aliud matrimonium contrahere, moecharique eum qui dimissa adultera alteram duxerit, et eam, quae dimisso adultero, alii nupserit,

> Anathema sit.

In order to properly appreciate the complexity of this teaching and to understand the impact of this teaching on subsequent Church tradition, it is important to study some of the specific words within Canon 7:

First, *errare:* the Council intended here to teach that it *is* within the Church's competence to deal with the question of

matrimony. This teaching was made explicit in order to coun-
teract the reformers' assertions which removed matrimony
from the realm of the supernatural.

Second, *iuxta:* there was debate within the Council about
whether or not at this point in Canon 7 to use the word *cum*
(with), *praeter* (beyond) or *iuxta* (according to). The Council
decided finally on the word *iuxta* in order to stress that the
teaching of Canon 7 was inspired by the Scriptures and tradition. In other words, the *iuxta* usage is to demonstrate that this
teaching of Canon 7 is "in line with" the teaching of the Gos-
pels and the apostles.

Karl Lehmann likewise interprets this *iuxta* to indicate
that the Tridentine formula is stating that the teaching and the
practice of the Western Church is "in accordance with *(juxta)*
the teaching of the Gospel."[6] In other words, the Western
practice regarding divorce is not simply *the* teaching of the
Gospel but Trent is leaving it open whether there are other
modes of response "in accordance with" Scripture.

Lehmann insists that the two lines of unbroken certainty
(Jesus' absolute requirement and the practice of toleration in
Paul and the Matthean church) are not simply parallel, as if
they were "equally justified." The principle of indissolubility,
then, claims an inherently higher normative force, while the
concessions are viewed, in Lehmann's terminology, as "not
entirely without foundation." The concessions thus have the
function of drawing attention to the obligatory character of
Jesus' directive. From this Lehmann concludes a key principle:

> *The concession of milder practice must not turn into*
> *an independent system, relatively or at least in fact*
> *indifferent to the principle of indissolubility. For it is*
> *outside the limits of what in faith indubitably ought*
> *to be the case, and consequently there is no place for*
> *it purely and simply in itself. There is, therefore, fun-*

damentally no intrinsic "right" to divorce, remarriage and eventual subsequent readmission to the sacraments.[7]

Third, *vinculum:* an earlier draft of Canon 7 simply stated that "the marriage cannot be dissolved." The Council eventually added the concept of *vinculum* to stress that "the bond" of marriage cannot be broken because of adultery: i.e., there is no such thing as "intrinsic dissolubility."

Gaudium et Spes of Vatican II, no. 49, repeats this same point:

Sealed by mutual faithfulness and hallowed above all by Christ's sacrament, this love remains steadfastly true in body and in mind, in bright days or dark. It will never be profaned by adultery or divorce.

It is precisely this juridical sense of *vinculum* which many authors presently feel must be reexamined, as we have already seen in Chapter Four:[8] i.e., whether it is the mutual consent or the commitment of love which constitutes the actual *vinculum* (bond) of marriage.

The Council of Trent also issued the Decree *Tametsi.* Since the proclamation of Pope Alexander III that marriage is constituted by consent, numerous clandestine marriages had arisen whereby the marital union was accomplished by the simple exchange of consent without any witnesses. Because of this historical problem, the reformers maintained that marriage without "parental consent" was invalid, and that parents could validate a marriage by consequent consent.

In order to resolve this historical difficulty, *Tametsi* declared that parental consent was not necessary for the validity of a marriage but that the banns of marriage had to be announced three times before the marriage itself (actually a reiteration of the prescription of the Fourth Lateran Council).

Tametsi likewise taught that persons who entered into clandestine marriages entered into invalid marriages. In this regard, the Council of Trent legislated the proper "form" of a valid marriage: i.e., marriage was to be witnessed by the *parochus* or by the priest delegated by him or by the bishop, and by two or three other witnesses.

The Council was careful to point out that this requirement affected the "contracting parties" rather than the contract itself. This particular point was important since many considered the contract itself to be the sacrament, over which the Church has only a protective and not a constitutive function.

To this day, this "form" of *Tametsi* normatively binds all Catholics. It is important to keep in mind, however, that the Code of Canon Law presents certain possible dispensations from this form: e.g., under certain circumstances a Catholic might be permitted to have his or her marriage witnessed in a non-Catholic ceremony.

Summary

This chapter has attempted to demonstrate the complexity of the issue of divorce within the history of the Church. We saw that up until the sixth century there was no definitive Christian position established on divorce and remarriage.

Numerous authors and councils of the Church wrestled with the concept of divorce, many upholding the right of a husband to divorce an adulterous wife.

This debate became more complex with the question of codification: i.e., what constitutes the matrimonial bond, mutual consent or carnal relations? Pope Alexander III resolved this debate by teaching that marriage is constituted by consent and that physical consummation adds a perfection to this consent, thus establishing absolute indissolubility.

The Council of Trent clearly defined marriage as one of the seven sacraments and clearly taught that intrinsic dissolubility does not and cannot exist: e.g., partners themselves dissolve the marriage because of adultery.

Finally, Trent established two essentially important facts that affect the Catholic understanding of marriage to this day: (a) the consent of the parties in marriage establishes an unbreakable *vinculum* (bond); (b) all Catholics are normatively bound to proper canonical form: i.e., a Catholic's marriage must be witnessed by a priest/deacon and at least two witnesses.

9

Pastoral Considerations

Overview

On September 10, 1987, Father Frank J. McNulty addressed Pope John Paul II in Miami as a representative of the United States priests. He began his presentation with this story:

After a large dinner at one of England's stately mansions, a famous actor entertained the guests with stunning Shakespearean readings. Then, as an encore, he offered to accept a request. A shy, grayhaired priest asked if he knew Psalm 23. The actor said, "Yes, I do and I will give it on one condition: that when I am finished you recite the very same Psalm."

The priest was a little embarrassed, but consented. The actor did a beautiful rendition: 'My shepherd is the Lord, there is nothing I shall want,' and so on. The guests applauded when the actor was done, and then it was the priest's turn. The man got up and said the same words, but this time there was no applause, just a hushed silence and the beginning of a tear in some eyes.

The actor savored the silence for a few moments and then stood up. He said, "Ladies and gentlemen, I

*hope you realized what happened here tonight. I
knew the Psalm, but this man knows the Shepherd."*[1]

Father McNulty used this story to express both the fact
and the hope that all priests be dedicated to knowing the Shepherd. This point could profitably be expanded to indicate that
the main thrust of ministry in the Church is assisting all men
and women to come to a deeper knowledge of and appreciation
for the Lord Jesus.

This book has dealt with numerous issues which touch
profoundly on the life of separated, divorced and remarried
Catholics. The Introduction to this work indicated that there
are important pastoral issues which this text has not addressed:
e.g., the emotional trauma that touches the life of every
divorced individual, and the difficulties regarding the nature of
a second marriage. It would be inopportune to conclude such
a volume, however, without articulating certain pastoral considerations that must be present in dealing with divorced and
remarried Catholics. Ministry in the Church necessarily entails
assisting men and women to faithfully know the Shepherd.
This posture must mark all attitudes of ministry in dealing with
those who struggle through the problems of separation,
divorce and remarriage.

While it is certainly possible to articulate clearly the
Church's theological position on numerous questions relating
to divorce and remarriage, viable ministry demands as a starting
point frank acknowledgement that problems do exist in this
whole area, perhaps even more on the practical than on the
theoretical level.[2] This book has attempted to affirm that there
are clear principles concerning the sacrament of marriage. At
the same time, however, it is equally important to acknowledge
that this affirmation occurs in a world affected by sin, that marriages do break down, and that persons involved in such tra-
gedies do turn to the Church for help. Chapter Two pointed

out that the stability of Christian marriages is anchored in God's fidelity. God's commitment is for the life of the spouses. The Church's ministry to those who suffer through the pains of separation, divorce and possible remarriage must be rooted in the same fidelity, aimed always toward the life of the actual women and men who suffer the difficulties of separation and divorce.

A Christian marriage can fail since a human person can fail. Ladislas Orsy, S. J. correctly writes:

> *A human person can be unfaithful to his covenant. He can turn away from God, and he can turn away from his partner....*
>
> *The result of such action is that the marriage comes to such a total collapse that none of the elements of its ordinary definition, "communion of life," consortium totius vitae, are verifiable anymore. It goes through a passage from being to apparent nonbeing. The institution brought into concrete existence by two persons tumbles down. Its ends are not fulfilled any more. No mutual help is given.*[3]

It is essential that the Church be viably present to any person where this "tumbling" has or is occurring. Once again, the words of Pope John II in *Familiaris Consortio* (1981) are vitally important:

> *... I earnestly call upon pastors and the whole community of the faithful to help the divorced and with solicitous care to make sure that they do not consider themselves as separated from the Church. ... Let the Church pray for them, encourage them and show*

herself a merciful mother and thus sustain them in
faith and hope. . . .

The process of ministry to the separated and divorced
Catholic must adopt, then, the same attitude that touched the
ministry of Jesus:

God in Christ was reconciling the world to himself,
not holding men's faults against them, and he has
entrusted to us the news that they are reconciled. So
we are ambassadors for Christ; it is as though God
were appealing to us, and the appeal that we make is:
Be reconciled to God (2 Cor 5:19–21).

Divorce-as-Process

All men and women who suffer the crisis of separation and
divorce, and even the trauma which is involved in remarriage,
truly need and deserve a pastoral care in the Church which
acknowledges the spiritual and psychological effects of pain,
while acknowledging the increased motivation that a crisis can
supply for the healing process:

The dis-ease of crisis exceeds emotional boundaries
and establishes a sensitive and vulnerable opening for
spiritual healing and wellness. Crisis, therefore,
becomes a teachable moment, a time for reconcilia-
tion when someone is more likely to accept God's
grace and invitation to resolve painful dilemmas and
restore or deepen one's relationships with self, fam-
ily, Church and God.[4]

The separated and divorced Catholic, then, should " . . .
not consider themselves as separated from the Church," but
realize as well that they have a tremendous gift to offer to the

Church as they suffer the profound and disturbing confusions which surround separation and divorce.

To enter into the suffering of the separated, divorced person, we need to understand the predictable stages of this trauma, patterned after Dr. Elisabeth Kübler-Ross' stages of death and dying[5] that the separating and divorcing person experiences at the death of the married relationship. These stages are not necessarily experienced in the order we will speak of them here, but in the vast majority of cases these experiences somehow touch all persons struggling through the difficulties of separation and divorce.

Additional problems arise in these "stages" when a person experiences exultation of moving out of one stage, feeling a sense of peace and success, only to be dashed back into a former experience of denial, depression, anger and so on. When there are children, for example, the "married relationship" seems forever reinforced at such events as graduations, weddings, births, funerals and traditional family gatherings.

In addition, even though each individual experiences these stages in uniquely personal ways, the timetable in general fits most people's experience, especially those who have been left rather than those who do the leaving. A correct notion of ministry cautions, however, that every individual recovers in his or her own time.

Before looking specifically at the various stages of death and dying experienced at the "tumbling" of the married relationship, it is also important to remember that civil dissolution (divorce) is much more complicated than the legal/civil aspects of the question. As demonstrated in Chapter One, divorce is never an easy solution to a difficult marriage; divorce is never easily chosen. Many times it is not chosen at all: it is imposed. Reputable studies more than sufficiently demonstrate that divorce is the *final* solution to an intolerable marriage; it is not the *first* answer.[6] Divorce is elected when other resources to resolve marital needs and conflicts have truly failed. In general, it is chosen with immense sadness and personal loss. It is one of the most difficult decisions a person faces, for its toll affects each family member.

The complexity of the question of divorce must be profoundly acknowledged in assisting divorced Catholics in their hope to "know the Shepherd" in ever deepening ways through and in the wrenching experiences of divorce.

The stages which we are about to outline demonstrate, for example, that divorce is not merely a legal dissolution, but even more profoundly an emotional trauma. In addition, children normally suffer in varied, complex ways through the trauma of divorce, and thus it is essential that authentic ministry in the Church provide sensitive avenues to assist children of separated and divorced Catholics.

As with death and dying, the separating and divorcing person might experience several of these stages at once or, as we have seen, repeat a stage in a new way because of stress or "reminders" of the previous marital relationship. What are these stages?

First: Denial. This stage includes feelings of shock: "This is not happening . . . " This stage likewise involves a profound sense of rejection: "I am no longer lovable." Inevitably, this stage in the process of dealing with separation and divorce likewise sustains elements of fear, panic, and embarrassment: "What will happen to me now?" and "I can't tell anyone about this—I am so ashamed."

Second: Depression. This stage entails an overwhelming and powerful feeling of being trapped in one's inner world of pain and suffering. A person at this stage usually senses and experiences an inner turmoil of helplessness, hopelessness, sadness, unworthiness, and perhaps even suicidal feelings. In this stage, it is very important in ministry to recall the "image" of depression which Sigmund Freud suggested: If one sits in a room staring intensely at a wall, it is quite possible to see something not quite perfect in that wall: e.g., a crack. It can happen that one's fixation on the crack can become so intense that in one's mind the crack grows larger and larger, and soon the wall is no longer seen. Depression then sets in, as a loss of perspective.

Unquestionably the crack is real and must be dealt with; but it is not the entire wall. During the stage of depression, it is of great importance to remind the individual of a possible "loss of perspective": i.e., one's life is filled with wonderful gifts and immense potential that is larger than the specific dimension of separation and divorce.

Depression can also result from the fear of being alone the rest of one's life, which causes some people actually to remain in a bad marriage rather than to face the unknown. For example, depression can be a major impetus which drives persons to the single-bar scene and toward the rebound marriage phenomenon that we saw in Chapter One.

This is precisely a time when the Church and its ministers need to recall the reconciling face of Jesus (2 Cor 5:19–21) and invite the alienated, wounded person into the healing and unconditional love of God.

Third: Anger. Anger usually focuses on several different aspects of the separation/divorce process. One can be angry, for example, at having loved and trusted the spouse so much. One can be angry in so many multiple ways: at the economic situation, at God for allowing this to happen, and at the Church which seems to some to be aloof and nonunderstanding. The testimony of one party in an annulment process clearly expresses this anger:

> *What I find very difficult to accept is that the Church attempts to perpetuate the feeling of guilt over something that occurred many years ago, and no matter*

*how good a Christian I am, I am not worthy enough
to receive Holy Communion. . . . It's a shame that the
Church cannot cut through its doctrine and get to the
point.*

Fourth: Bargaining. This point in the process is an attempt
to postpone or change the present stressful situation by bargaining with God, with the partner, or with oneself to get the
spouse to change or to return.

Fifth: Acceptance. This point in the process comes only
after a long-term effort. It comes gradually as one lets go of the
past expectation of a lifelong, intact family. This stage is of
utmost importance, however, to allow a new beginning in
one's life to emerge, a point where an individual again feels "in
charge" of one's life. It is important to remember that this
stage does not mean forgetting the past, but it does mean allowing the past to be present in one's life in such a way as to be a
healing impetus rather than a destructive force.

Sixth: Recovery. This stage has special religious and
moral aspects as one learns that it is truly only God who
empowers one to transform the wounds of life into new and
viable opportunities. This time-recovery takes a great deal of
patience, evaluation and readjustment. It takes the courage to
develop a new, single identity.

These stages have been witnessed time and again by
numerous persons ministering to the separated and divorced
Catholic. The work of the North American Conference of
Separated and Divorced Catholics (NACSDC) affirms that the
trauma of divorce entails the following experiences for the
majority of Catholics:

(1) A deep sense of a "break" with oneself, the marriage part-
    ner, family, God and the Church.

(2) Intense, emotional responses, especially those of guilt, failure and shame.

(3) Overwhelming fear or actual experience of abandonment or rejection by loved ones, local church, institutional Church.

(4) Belief that one has grievously sinned by going against the teachings of the Church about marriage.

(5) Disassociation from parish because of real or perceived rejection or excommunication.

(6) Severe anxiety about one's future heightened by the fear that the Church mandates "aloneness" in its teaching about remarriage.

(7) Concerns about children who might become disaffected from the sacraments or who might be labeled "illegitimate" as a result of their parents' divorce status.

These experiences of confusion, anguish and trauma certainly demonstrate the various stages of dying and death experienced by separated and divorced Catholics. In assisting these persons to "know the Shepherd," it is obviously important for the Church and its ministers to be sensitive to the whole process which one suffers in dealing with a failed marriage.

Ministry in the Church

A growing number of parishes in the United States are growing ever more attuned to the anxieties and problems suffered by separated and divorced Catholics. Parishes are demonstrating a profound concern and ministry to these persons, a concern which is truly rooted in the compassionate and reconciling posture of Jesus, the Good Shepherd.

The "Preamble" of the North American Conference of Separated and Divorced Catholics might well conclude this book by marking the attitude of respect and reverence which we all must adopt in ministering to those who suffer from separation and divorce:

> *We . . . dedicate ourselves to develop and expand the peer ministry within the Catholic community that offers encouragement, support and education to all who experience separation and divorce. While affirming always our traditional Catholic teaching and values on marriage and family life, we recognize with sadness that some Catholics may need to divorce and should then receive effective pastoral care from the Church. Further, we strive to create greater awareness among the separated and divorced that their anguish can become a source of new personal and spiritual growth for themselves and a source of grace for the whole community. We also endeavor to create greater awareness within the Church community that the pain and growth experienced by the separated and divorced person can enhance the Church's understanding of marriage as a sacrament and suffering as a Christian reality. As separated, divorced and remarried Catholics, we invite the whole faith community to recognize and learn from our unique experience and to affirm that all separated, divorced and remarried Catholics do truly belong within and have much to offer the Church community.*[7]

Summary

In this concluding chapter on "Pastoral Considerations," we have attempted to demonstrate that all ministry in the Church must be rooted in a dedication to assist others to come to "know the Shepherd" in ever-more viable and profound ways. This dedication is rooted in the affirmation that there are firm and clear principles in the Church concerning the sacrament of marriage. At the same time, there must be the frank acknowledgement that because of sin, human frailty and weaknesses, problems do exist, marriages do break down, and Catholics turn to the Church for ministry and for help.

In his *Apostolic Exhortation on the Family* (1981), Pope John Paul II strongly urges the whole Catholic community to assist the separated and divorced with "solicitous care." Pastoral exigency demands that we pursue this counsel with vitality, hope and reconciling encouragement.

We have seen in Chapters One and Two, as well as in this chapter, that divorce is never an easy choice and always brings trauma, anxiety and pain. The stages of dying and death suggested by Dr. Elisabeth Kübler-Ross are helpful and instructive in dealing with those suffering through the process of separation and divorce. A poignant image in Scripture is that of Matthew 9:35–36:

> *Jesus went about all the cities and villages, teaching . . . and preaching . . . and healing . . . every infirmity. When he saw the crowds, he had compassion for them, because they were harassed and helpless like sheep without a Shepherd.*

The passion to heal was central in Jesus, and must be central in the Church's ministry to the separated and divorced Catholic.

In *Prayer, Stress, and Our Inner Wounds*,[8] Flora Slosson Wuellner beautifully portrays the healing Jesus:

> *A picture that was hung in my room when I was a child changed my life. It was a picture of a shepherd climbing down a rugged cliffside; with one hand he gripped a rock and with the other he reached down*

to a sheep that had fallen to a ledge below. Its face looked up in terror and trust. A bird of prey circled overhead. I could not see the shepherd's face as he strained down to the sheep, but I could see the knotted muscles, the bleeding hands and arms gnashed by thorns, the twisted garment torn in the steep descent. . . .

I stared in amazement. This picture was very different from the one of the Good Shepherd on the wall of my Sunday school room. In that one a placid shepherd in a spotless white robe strolled along a grassy level path, carrying an equally spotless and placid lamb.

The shepherd in my picture was paying a real and painful price. I could see from the concentrated body and the compassionate authority of the outstretched hand that to reach the hurt and crying animal mattered more to him than anything else in the world. And I knew as I gazed at the picture that the sheep would be reached, held, healed and lifted to life.[9]

Bibliography

Atkinson, David John, *To Have and To Hold: The Marriage Covenant and the Discipline of Divorce*, Grand Rapids, Mich.: Eerdmans, 1981.

Baruth, Leroy G., *A Single Parent's Survival Guide*, Dubuque, Iowa: Kendall/Hunt Publishing Co., 1979.

Berger, T., *How Does It Feel When Your Parents Get Divorced?* New York: J. Messner, 1977.

Berman, Claire G., *Stepfamilies—A Growing Reality*, New York: Public Affairs Committee, 1982.

————, *What Am I Doing in a Stepfamily?* New Jersey: Lyle Smart, 1982.

————, *Making It as a Stepparent: New Roles/New Rules*, New York: Doubleday, 1980.

Briggs, Dorothy Corkille, *Your Child's Self-Esteem*, New York: Doubleday and Co., 1975.

Carpenter, S., Frawner, E., O'Brien, G., and Waugh, P., *Learning To Live Again*, Cincinnati, Ohio: St. Anthony Messenger Press, 1979.

Castelli, J., *What the Church Is Doing for Divorced and Remarried Catholics*, Chicago, Ill.: Claretian Publications, 1978.

Cherlin, Andrew J., *Marriage, Divorce, Remarriage: Changing Patterns in the Postwar United States*, Cambridge: Harvard University Press, 1981.

Despert, M.D., J. Louise, *Children of Divorce*, New York: Doubleday & Co., 1953.

DiGiulio, Robert C., *When You Are a Single Parent*, St. Meinrad, Ind.: Abbey Press, 1979.

Doherty, Dennis, *Divorce and Remarriage: Resolving a Catholic Dilemma,* St. Meinrad, Ind.: Abbey Press, 1974.

Ferm, Dean W., *Alternative Lifestyles Confront the Church,* Minneapolis: Winston/Seabury Publication, 1983.

Ford, Edward E., *Choosing To Love: A New Way To Respond,* Minneapolis: Winston/Seabury Publications, 1983.

Furstenberg, Frank F. and Spanier, Graham B., *Recycling the Family: Remarriage After Divorce,* Beverly Hills, Cal.: Sage Publications, Inc., 1984.

Gardner, M.D., Richard A., *Psychotherapy with Children of Divorce,* New York: Jason Aronson, 1976.

————, *The Boys and Girls Book About Divorce,* New York: Bantam Books, 1971.

————, *The Boys and Girls Book About Stepfamilies,* New York: Bantam Books, 1985.

————, *The Parents Book About Divorce,* New York: Bantam Books, 1977.

Greeley, A. M., *The Young Catholic Family: Religious Images and Marital Fulfillment,* Chicago: The Thomas More Press, 1980.

Greteman, Jim, *Coping with Divorce,* Notre Dame, Ind.: Ave Maria Press, 1984.

Grollman, Earl, *Explaining Divorce to Children,* New York: Beacon Press, 1969.

————, *Living Through Your Divorce,* Boston: Beacon Press, 1978.

————, *Talking About Divorce and Separation,* Boston: Beacon Press, 1975.

Hunt, Morton and Hunt, Bernice, *The Divorce Experience,* New York: The New American Library, Inc., 1977.

Kelleher, Stephen Joseph, *Divorce and Remarriage for Catholics?* Garden City, N.Y.: Doubleday, 1973.

Kelly, Kevin T., *Divorce and Second Marriages—Facing the Challenge,* New York: Seabury Press, 1983.

Klein, Carole, *The Single Parent Experience*, New York: Avon Books, 1973.

Kushner, Robert C., *When Bad Things Happen to Good People*, New York: Schocken Books, 1981.

Laz, Medard, *Helps for the Separated and Divorced*, Liguori, Mo.: Liguori Publications, 1981.

Lorimer, A. and Feldman, P., *Remarriage, a Guide for Singles, Couples, and Families, Including Stepchildren, In-laws, Ex-Spouses, Possessions, Housing, Finances, and More*, Philadelphia: Running Press, 1980.

Mackin, S. J., Theodore, *Divorce and Remarriage*, New York: Paulist Press, 1984.

Mann, P., *My Dad Lives in a Downtown Hotel*, Garden City, N.Y.: Doubleday & Co., 1973.

McRoberts, D. B., *Second Marriage*, Minneapolis: Augsburg Publishing House, 1978.

O'Brien, Judith T., and O'Brien, Gene, *A Redeeming State: A Handbook—Leaders' Guide for Couples Planning Remarriage in the Church*, Mahwah, N.J.: Paulist Press, 1984.

Pospishil, Victor J., *Divorce and Remarriage: Towards a New Catholic Teaching*, New York: Herder and Herder, 1967.

Preister, Steven and Young, James J., eds., *Catholic Remarriage: Pastoral Issues and Preparation Models*, Mahwah, N.J.: Paulist Press, 1986.

Ricci, Isolina, *Mom's House, Dad's House*, New York: Macmillan Publishing Co., 1980.

Ripple, Paula, *The Pain and the Possibility: Divorce and Separation Among Catholics*, Notre Dame, Ind.: Ave Maria Press, 1978.

————, *Walking With Loneliness*, Notre Dame, Ind.: Ave Maria Press, 1982.

Rue, James J., *A Catechism for Divorced Catholics*, St. Meinrad, Ind.: Abbey Press, 1976.

Rue, James J. and Shanahan, Louise, *The Divorced Catholic*, Mahwah, N.J.: Paulist Press, 1972.

————, *The Limbo World of the Divorced*, Chicago: Franciscan Herald Press, 1979.

Sell, Kenneth D., *Divorce in the 70's: A Subject Bibliography*, Phoenix: Oryx Press, 1981.

Spaniol, LeRoy J. and Lannan, Paul A., *Getting Unstuck: Moving On After a Divorce*, New York: Paulist Press, 1984.

Twomey, Gerald S., *When Catholics Marry Again: A Guide for the Divorced, Their Families and Those Who Minister to Them*, Minneapolis, Minn.: Winston Press, 1982.

Visher, Emily and John, *Stepfamilies—Myths and Realities*, New York: Citadel Press, 1980.

Weiss, Robert S., *Marital Separation: Coping with the End of a Marriage and the Transition to Being Single Again*, New York: Basic Books, 1975.

Wrenn, Lawrence G., *Divorce and Remarriage in the Catholic Church*, New York: Newman Press, 1973.

Young, James J., ed., *Divorce Ministry and the Marriage Tribunal*, New York: Paulist Press, 1982.

————, *Divorcing, Believing, Belonging*, New York: Paulist Press, 1984.

————, *Growing Through Divorce*, New York: Paulist Press, 1979.

————, *Ministering to the Divorced Catholic*, New York: Paulist Press, 1979.

Zwack, Joseph, *Annulments, Your Chance to Remarry in the Catholic Church*, New York: Harper and Row, 1983.

Notes

Introduction

1. See Lawrence G. Wrenn, "Marriage—Indissoluble or Fragile?" in *Divorce and Remarriage in the Catholic Church*, ed. Lawrence G. Wrenn, New York: Newman Press, 1973, 144–145.

2. For a good review of recent literature, see "Divorce as a Pastoral Problem" in "Notes on Moral Theology," Richard A. McCormick, S.J., *Theological Studies* 41 (1980), 123–138.

3. *Gaudium et Spes*, no. 48.

4. *Lumen Gentium*, no. 11. In Ireland, e.g., Archbishop Kevin McNamara vigorously opposed efforts to liberalize the nation's divorce laws. When the state permits second and third marriages in violation of the commandments of God and the Church, he argued, it cloaks these morally unlawful unions with a kind of legitimacy that leads society eventually to accept marriage as provisional rather than permanent.

5. For a good treatment of these issues, see Paula Ripple, *The Pain and the Possibility*, Notre Dame: Ave Maria Press, 1978; and Reva Wiseman, "Crises Theory and the Process of Divorce," *Social Casework* 56 (1975), 205–212.

6. Walter Kasper, *Theology of Christian Marriage*, New York: Crossroad, 1980, 67.

7. *Ibid.*, 67–68.

1. Divorce and Remarriage: The People

1. See James J. Young, "Remarried Catholics Searching for Church Belonging," and Steven Preister, "Marriage,

Divorce and Remarriage in the United States," *New Catholic World* 229 (1986), 4–8 and 9–19.

2. Preister, 9–19; see especially 19 for abundant statistical studies.

3. *Ibid.*, 11.

4. *Ibid.*, 13.

5. *Ibid.*

6. *Familiaris Consortio*, no. 84.

7. In October 1983 the Holy See issued its "Charter of the Rights of the Family." This Charter also upholds the centrality of the family and the marital bond. The Charter teaches in Article 1, e.g., that "the institutional value of marriage should be upheld by the public authorities; the situation of non-married couples must not be placed on the same level of marriage duly contracted." And in Article 6, it teaches that "divorce attacks the very institution of marriage and of the family."

2. Marriage: A Catholic Perspective

1. See F. Nietzsche, *Genealogy of Morals*, II, ed. S. Schlechta, Munich, 1955, 799.

2. See G. Marcel, *Mystere de l'Etre*, Vienna, 1952, 472.

3. We will here summarize the excellent analysis of Christian marriage as given by Walter Kasper in *Theology of Christian Marriage*, New York: Crossroad, 1980, 9–24.

4. See Denis J. Doherty, "Childfree Marriage: A Theological View," *Chicago Studies* 18 (1979), 137–145.

5. See William J. Lederer and Don D. Jackson, "The Eight Myths of Marriage," *New Woman* 141 (1975), 67–71.

6. See *Gaudium et Spes*, no. 4ff.

7. *Gaudium et Spes*, no. 48.

8. *Gaudium et Spes*, no. 25.

9. Kasper, 30.

10. *Lumen Gentium*, no. 11.

11. See Thomas P. Doyle, "The Church and Marital Breakdown," *New Catholic World* 229 (1986), 23–31.

3. The Faith Dimension

1. See Susan Wood, S.C.L., "The Marriage of Baptized Nonbelievers: Faith, Contract, and Sacrament," *Theological Studies* 48 (1987), 279–301. This article superbly analyzes the many questions surrounding the area of "living faith." In this chapter, we will follow a great deal of the excellent presentation of Wood.

2. See *Origins* 8 (1978), 200–204.

3. See Kasper, *op. cit.,* 81–83.

4. D.S. 794, 1262, 1313, 1611.

5. See Thomas Aquinas, *Summa Theologiae* III, 64, 9 ad. 1.

6. See *Official Catholic Teaching Update 1978*, Wilmington, N.C.: McGrath and Co., 1980, 150.

7. See, for example, R. Cunningham, "Marriage and the Nescient Catholic: Questions of Faith and Sacrament," *Studia canonica* 15 (1981); and Walter Cuenin, "Marriage and Baptized Non-Believers—Questions: Faith, Sacrament and Law," *Origins* 8 (1978); and Edward J. Kilmartin, "When Is Marriage a Sacrament?" *Theological Studies* 34 (1973).

8. See *Origins* 8 (1977–1978), 235ff.

9. Wood, 290–293.

10. *Ibid.,* 291.

11. See St. Thomas, 4 Sent, d. 39, q. 1, a. 1, ad 5.

12. Karl Rahner, "Atheism and Implicit Christianity," *Theology Digest* 16 (1968) 43–56.

13. Karl Rahner, *Nature and Grace,* New York: Sheed and Ward, 1964, chapter 5; and "Marriage as a Sacrament," *Theological Investigations* 10, New York: Seabury Press, 1977, 204ff.

14. Wood, 300.

15. *Ibid.*, 292–293.

16. Canon 1063.

17. Pope Paul VI, *Sacerdotalis Caelibatus*, 1967, no. 64.

4. Eucharistic Participation

1. John Paul II, *Redemptor Hominis*, March 4, 1979, no. 20.

2. *Origins* 6 (1976–1977), 765–766.

3. Joseph M. Powers, S.J., *New Catholic World* 229 (1986), 37–42.

4. *Ibid.*, 40.

5. *Constitution on the Sacred Liturgy*, no. 14.

6. *Pastoral Constitution on the Church in the Modern World*, no. 38.

7. *La Documentation Catholique* 76 (1979), 715–722, nos. 21–31.

8. Pope Paul VI, "The Marriage Bond," *The Pope Speaks* 21 (1976), 152–153.

9. See, for example, Charles M. Whelan, S.J. "Divorced Catholics," *America* 131 (1974), 363–365; James J. Young, ed., *Ministering to the Divorced Catholic*, New York: Paulist Press, 1979; James Provost, "Reconciliation of Catholics in Second Marriages," *Origins* 8 (1978–1979), 204–208.

10. See Gerald D. Coleman, S.S., "Participation in the Eucharist by Those in an Irregular Marriage," *The Priest* 14 (1982) 36–41.

11. "Christological Theses on the Sacrament of Marriage," *Origins* 8 (1978–1979), 200–204, citation here at 203–204. A question often raised in this regard of "countersign" and "counterwitness" is the Church's admittance of non-Catholics to the Eucharist: see "On Admitting Other Christians to Eucharistic Communion in the Catholic Church" (1 June 1972) and "Note Interpreting the 'Instruction on Admitting

Other Christians to Eucharistic Communion in the Catholic Church Under Certain Circumstances'" (October 17, 1973). It must be noted in this regard that this admittance is considered "rare" and certain conditions are necessary in order for a diocesan bishop to grant such permission: for example, faith in this sacrament in conformity with that of the Church, an experienced need for the spiritual sustenance of the Eucharist, a prolonged period where recourse to one's own minister is not possible, and correct dispositions of a worthy life.

5. The Internal Forum Solution

1. "Forum," *Sacramentum Mundi,* ed. Karl Rahner, Vol. 2, New York: Herder and Herder, 1968, 344–346.

2. See, for example, James J. Young, "Remarried Catholics Searching for Church Belonging," *New Catholic World* 229 (1986), 4–8.

3. Henry Noldin, *De Poenitentiae,* q. 3, a. 2. Pertinent to this discussion as well is the April 4, 1977 publication of Cardinal Felici, "Juridical Formalities and the Evaluation of the Proofs in a Canonical Process." This paper is speaking about the "good faith" of a tribunal judge and the necessity for the judge to have "moral certitude" regarding decisions reached, proofs which the judge must weigh *ex sua conscientia.* Felici underlines this point in order to distinguish "moral certitude" from "rigid formalism."

4. For a fuller explanation, see Gerald D. Coleman, S.S., "The Internal Forum Solution," *The Priest* 39 (1983), 33–36.

5. *Familiaris Consortio* (1982), no. 84.

6. The Question of Excommunication

1. Peter Guilday, *A History of the Councils of Baltimore (1791–1884),* New York: The Macmillan Company, 1932, 142.

2. It is important to recall that Baltimore became an Archdiocese in 1809, with four suffragans: Boston, New York, Philadelphia, and Bardstown, Kentucky (later, Louisville). Baltimore retained this geographical jurisdiction until 1850, when New York was made an Archdiocese. The Province of Baltimore thus ran from the Canadian border to Florida (excluded) and from the Atlantic Ocean to the Mississippi River.

3. Pastoral Letter of the Third Council of Baltimore, 1884, no. 2.

4. The Third Council of Baltimore, 1884, Statute no. 124.

5. See Bouscaren, Ellis, Korth, *Canon Law: A Text and Commentary*, New York: Macmillan Company, 1963, 964.

6. *Ibid.*, 811. In the new Code, see 1313–1320 and 1323.

7. Canon 1323:2,4.

8. L. C. Farley, "Immediate Internal Forum Solution," *The Jurist* 30 (1970), 73. See also Gerald P. Fogarty, S.J., "The Historical Origin of the Excommunication of Divorced and Remarried Catholics Imposed by the Third Plenary Council of Baltimore," *The Jurist* 38 (1978), 426–433; William May, "Marriage, Divorce, and Remarriage," *The Jurist* 37 (1977), 266–286; James H. Provost, "Intolerable Marriage Situations Revisited," *The Jurist* 40 (1980), 141–196; and Francisco Javier Urrutia, S.J., "The 'Internal Forum Solution'—Some Comments," *The Jurist* 40 (1980), 128–140.

7. Scriptural Data

1. Joseph A. Fitzmyer, S.J., "The Matthean Divorce Texts and Some New Palestinian Evidence," *Theological Studies* 37 (1976), 197–226, here at 224.

2. Bruce Vawter, "The Divorce Question," *Catholic Biblical Quarterly* 29 (1977), 542.

3. Victor J. Pospishil, *Divorce and Remarriage*, New York: Herder and Herder, 1967, 37.

4. We will follow here the basic exegetical work of Joseph A. Fitzmyer, S.J., *op. cit.* and John P. Meier, *Christ, Church and Morality in the First Gospel,* New York: Paulist Press, 1978, esp. 248–257.

5. Steven Preister, *op. cit.,* 18.

8. Divorce in History

1. Karl Lehmann, "Indissolubility of Marriage and Pastoral Care of the Divorced Who Remarry," *Communio* 1 (1974), 219–242.

2. See, for example, Bernard Haering, *The Law of Christ* I, Maryland: Westminster, 1960, 403 ff.

3. Richard A. McCormick, S.J., *Theological Studies* 36 (1975), 103.

4. John T. Noonan, Jr., "Novel 22," in William W. Bassett, ed., *The Bond of Marriage,* Notre Dame: The University of Notre Dame Press, 1968, 41–96.

5. See Victor J. Pospishil, *Divorce and Remarriage,* New York: Herder and Herder, 1967, 51–52.

6. Karl Lehmann, *op. cit.,* 219.

7. *Ibid.,* 234.

8. See, for example, Richard A. McCormick, S.J., *op. cit.,* 112–113.

9. Pastoral Considerations

1. Frank J. McNulty, "A U.S. Priest Addresses the Pope," *Origins* 17 (1987), 231–234.

2. For a good discussion of this point, see Ladislas Orsy, S.J., "The Issue of Indissolubility: An Inquiry," *Thought* 59 (1984), 360–372.

3. *Ibid.,* 365.

4. The North American Conference of Separated and Divorced Catholics (NACSDC), *The Vocation and Mission of*

the Laity in the Church and in Society, New York: NACSDC, 1987, 4.

5. See Elisabeth Kübler-Ross, *On Death and Dying,* New York: The Macmillan Publishing Co., Inc., 1973; Reva Wiseman, "Crisis Theory and the Process of Divorce," *Social Casework* 56 (1975), 205–212.

6. *The Vocation and Mission of the Laity in the Church and in Society,* 14–15.

7. *Ibid.,* Preamble.

8. Flora Slosson Wuellner, *Prayer, Stress, and Our Inner Wounds,* Nashville: The Upper Room, 1985.

9. *Ibid.,* 11.

Subject Index